MAKING
CHANGES
LAST

MAKING CHANGES LAST

Jeffrey A. Kottler, Ph.D.

Routledge
Taylor & Francis Group
New York   London

First pubished by BRUNNER/MAZEL Philadelphia and London

This edition published 2012 by Routledge

Routledge   Routledge
Taylor & Francis Group   Taylor & Francis Group
711 Third Avenue   27 Church Road
New York, NY 10017   Hove East Sussex BN3 2FA

MAKING CHANGES LAST

Cover design by Ellen Seguin. Image courtesy of Jeffrey A. Kottler.

A CIP catalog record for this book is available from the British Library.

Library of Congress Cataloging-in-Publication Data

Kottler, Jeffrey A.
    Making changes last / Jeffrey A. Kottler.
      p. cm.
    Includes bibliographical references and index.
    ISBN 1-58391-086-7 (alk. paper)
    1. Change (Psychology) I. Title.
  BF637.C4 K68 2001
  155.2'5--dc21   2001025122

ISBN 1-58391-086-7 (paper)

CONTENTS

PREFACE

For most of my professional life I have been interested in how to make changes last. I have sat in rooms with people dripping with despair who beseeched me for help after their third relapse. I have listened to others promise over and over again that *this* time will be different: finally, they will take charge of their lives. I have watched helplessly while those I care about struggle courageously to gain a foothold of control or dignity, only to slip back a few weeks later. They feel dispirited and hopeless. So do I.

As a therapist and educator, I am interested in how to make changes last in my work. Far more than that, I am curious about how *any* transformative experience can be maintained throughout a lifetime, building on what was learned. During travel experiences, for example, it is interesting how some trips structured in a particular way lead to permanent lifestyle changes. Just as curious are the times in which people on vacation (or at conferences) vow to make dramatic changes in their lives but, once they return, resume their previous patterns. After two weeks, they have nothing to show for the holiday except for a few souvenirs and an exorbitant credit card bill.

☐ When Changes Last

"I know I can do it," Marilyn said to me with a voice whose force I found a little frightening. "I *will* do it," she continued, bobbing her head up and down like one of those dolls in the back window of a car. She was so convincing that I found my own head nodding in agreement. I almost believed her, but I knew better.

This was a client I had been seeing in therapy for almost a year who originally consulted me because she felt confused about what to do about her relationship with her boyfriend.

"He's no good for me, I know" she whimpered in a tone of voice that left me wondering whether she really agreed with what she was saying.

"I mean, I love him and all, but he just makes me feel so bad about myself."

I was hardly surprised. Marilyn had just related to me the recent story of her last visit to her boyfriend's house. He had insisted that she strip and get on her hands and knees in front of the television so he could mount her from behind while he watched the football game. At one point, he perched a bowl of popcorn on her back so he could enjoy a snack while he pounded away at her, hooting at the action on the screen.

I felt such revulsion at this scene that I wanted to strangle this guy I had never met. How could this lovely woman, with so much going for her, allow herself to be treated this way? I was determined to help her extricate herself from this abusive situation, or at the very least, to renegotiate the rules.

During each session we would review the meaning of this relationship in her life and how it was part of an ongoing pattern that began with her father when she was quite young. During the course of our dialogues, we investigated the origins of the abuse, uncovered long dormant memories, reviewed the history of her romantic affiliations (which resembled the current one), and explored the consequences of her predicament—how it impacted other life choices and self-perceptions.

After each of our sessions, Marilyn would summarize what she learned about herself, thank me profusely for my brilliant interventions and unwavering support, and then she would promptly return to the same dysfunctional behavior. She would end each meeting with the promise, "*This* week it's going to be different. I'm finally going to end it once and for all!"

I would then smile encouragingly and shrug. "It's up to you," I'd remind her, not believing for a minute that anything fundamental would be different in her life: "You will change things when you're ready."

While this prediction was certainly accurate, I wondered once again about the challenges of making changes last. Heck, it's easy to shake things up; the really hard part is keeping the momentum going. For some reason, Marilyn, and so many other clients who want to make lasting changes, are never able to pass whatever thresholds are in place that act to inhibit permanent transformation.

I felt so helpless with Marilyn and others like her: drug addicts, alcoholics, chronic smokers, and those with impulse disorders, severe personality disorders, or dysfunctional relationships. I felt like a fraud—or worse—a drug dealer. Maybe I was bringing only temporary relief, making people dependent on my services for their continued well-being.

Yet there were many others I had seen, and people I had known, who had indeed made lasting changes that continue to this day. I remember one cocaine addict who came for a single session. I told him there was nothing I could do for him. There was no cure. He was doomed. He would have to lose his wife, his children, his job, and all his money (hit bottom) before there might be hope. The guy must have believed me because he gave up his addiction on the spot, and he was still drug-free when I last checked up on him.

Sometimes I wonder whether the occasional dramatic and lasting change is just a fluke. But then I take inventory of others who have persisted in their efforts. Greg gave up smoking, for once and forever, after developing a serious bronchial condition. Melanie ended a 10-year disastrous marriage with an abusive man, her third in a row, and then finally linked up with a healthy partner in a relationship that still continues to grow in love and respect. I began running and eating a healthy diet the day after my mother died twenty-five years ago. I never looked back, or even felt tempted to relapse. Well, maybe a little.

The processes operating with those who make permanent changes in their lives do seem qualitatively different from the mechanisms involved with those whose changes do not persist. It would, therefore, be an extremely important mission for us to not only study ways to promote change in people's lives, but also to make the effects last.

☐ Where We Are Headed And Who This Book Is For

There are already so many tens of thousands of books about change that we hardly need another. Self-help books for the public are among the fastest growing segments of the publishing industry. Professional therapists, including psychiatrists, psychologists, social workers, family therapists, psychiatric nurses, addictions specialists, counselors, and mental health workers have an insatiable appetite for new volumes that offer some guidance in a very confusing and stressful field. Teachers, consultants, and other change agents also search continuously for improved ways to do their jobs.

People come to us in pain—desperate, hopeless, even suicidal—and they demand help. These people want to know what we can do for them. They want answers. And they want them quickly.

This book is not so much about change in therapy, or in *any* facet of life in which personal transformation takes place, but about what maintains and supports such growth. Whether we are looking at someone who leaves therapy a profoundly different person, or someone who makes similar changes as a result of travel, a book, a serendipitous encounter with a stranger, or a moment of revelation during a walk in the park, there is something remarkable that occurs during this process.

A number of questions that immediately come to mind are discussed in this book:

- What *is* change and how do you know when it occurs?
- When and why do people want to change?
- How and why does change take place?
- What are the different kinds of change?
- What are the differences between little and big changes?
- Why don't some changes last?
- Why are habits and addictions so frequently subject to relapses?
- Which conditions will most likely lead to lasting change?
- From where does sustained motivation originate?
- What can be done when nothing else seems to work?

These are questions that are pondered not only by the most experienced practitioners, but also by those who are new to the field. Students in introductory courses, as well as those studying theory and advanced practice, will find it extremely useful to examine the bigger picture of how changes take place in people's lives. This book is written for professional helpers who are interested in being more effective in their efforts to promote lasting changes—not only in their clients, but in their own lives as well.

You have heard enough empty promises in your life, especially from experts and authors, who say that all you have to do (which already sets off doubt) is follow their advice or foolproof plan, and deliverance will be just around the corner. Regardless of how you are already doing therapy (and the main message is that you are probably doing it wrong unless you modify your strategies to fit their new, improved model), this book seeks to help you become more knowledgeable and skilled at making the impact of your methods last longer. Rather than selling a particular ideology, the goal of this volume is to help you to examine the ways that change persists in a variety of contexts and make adjustments in the ways you work with clients in order to capitalize on the most potent effects.

☐ Acknowledgements

I wish to thank Tim Julet, my editor at Brunner/Routledge, for his continuing support and clear-headed guidance. I am also indebted to Fred Bemak, Richard Hazler, and Howard Rosenthal for reviewing the manuscript and making several suggestions for improving the book. I wish to thank

Maggie Yangye Li for help with the research for this book, both in the library and in the field. Finally, I am grateful for the openness of so many people who agreed to be interviewed for this project and to tell their stories of lasting change.

Jeffrey A. Kottler
Fullerton, California
June 2001

What Do We Really Understand About Change?

People constantly make resolutions about ending relationships or beginning new ones, ceasing bad habits, giving up addictions, changing jobs, and stopping self-destructive patterns. Efforts are initiated to get things rolling. Yet, so often, the changes just don't last.

The challenge of promoting and maintaining permanent change is one that befuddles experts, as well as the general public. Even professional change agents such as therapists, teachers, consultants, and business leaders struggle with ways to maintain progress that has been attained, as well as to prevent relapses—not only in their clients but in themselves.

Stop Me Before I Do It Again

I have resolved numerous times to handle certain situations in class differently, such as when a student rambles incessantly. I know from past experience that confronting such a person publicly, even in the most diplomatic, low-key way possible, often creates more problems than it solves. Even if the rambler does take my cue without feeling resentful, others in the class often feel vicariously censured.

Maybe it has something to do with my confrontive style, the students' need for approval, or some other factors I can't begin to understand, but I have accepted that I am just not as skilled as I would like to be in handling these annoying critical incidents. It is for this reason that I have promised myself over and over again that I won't use direct, public confrontation for these situations any longer but will, instead, rely on alternative means.

The problem, however, is that I quite enjoy being direct and I'm good at identifying behaviors that are counterproductive (except sometimes my own). So, as much as I understand that I must change my interventions, I feel powerless to do so. I keep repeating the exact same routines that get me in trouble. Furthermore, time and time again, I notice the same pattern with the therapists I supervise: we keep doing things that don't work very well but do them anyway because we don't seem to be able to stop. Furthermore, it often feels like we can't help ourselves.

☐ The Prognosis

We are often not all that honest with ourselves, much less with our clients, about the realistic prognosis for lasting change as a result of our helping efforts. There may be heaps of evidence to support the effectiveness of our interventions, but precious little to measure their sustained impact over long periods of time.

Steps Forward and Backward

All too often, people who wish to end destructive or self-defeating behaviors, cease bad habits, or make major lifestyle transformations do not persist in their efforts. In the case of addictions, for example, up to 80% of participants in recovery programs relapse, two thirds of them within three months (Hunt, & Barnett, & Branch, 1971; Laws, 1999). Lest you think this is a result of a population notably weak in impulse control, consider that in studies of high-functioning adults who make New Year's resolutions to stop smoking, lose weight, or begin exercise programs, 75% of them experienced success for the first week, but then, fully, 60% of the sample relapsed within six months (Norcross, Ratzin, & Payne, 1989). Considering that these people were prepared to receive follow-up calls from the researchers, even this result is optimistic.

These studies, as well as research conducted on the outcomes related to treatment of addictions and impulse control conclude that "there is no reason to expect that the effects of a treatment designed to moderate or to eliminate an undesirable behavior will necessarily persist for very long beyond the termination of that treatment" (Laws, 1995, p. 447). In other words, rather than fully expecting that our clients will maintain their progress after they leave our offices, it is far more reasonable to assume that the changes will probably not last.

How many times have you attended a workshop and were absolutely delighted with the material presented and determined to integrate what you learned in your practice, but found that a few weeks later you forgot most of what you learned? How many times have you participated in a retreat or intensive group experience and discovered that the glow lasted only about three days after you returned to daily pressures? How often have you gone on vacation or taken a break to rejuvenate yourself and found that whatever rest you experienced or goals you attained were completely nullified within a week after your return? More often than not, whether in therapy, on vacation, or during moments of quiet reflection, changes initiated do not persist without considerable preparation, rehearsal, and support.

Counseling, therapy, and workshop experiences are specifically structured to promote personal transformations and major growth. As such, they may be effective in producing positive results, but not nearly as successful in making the outcomes last. Before long, people often resume their maladaptive behaviors, bad habits, and destructive relationships. This might be very good for therapists, teachers, self-help writers, and other change agents who get lots of repeat customers, but it becomes an extremely frustrating and discouraging situation for those who would desperately like to move more than one step forward before they take another step backwards.

Keeping Resolutions

The general public is not the only group confused by the challenges of making changes last. Therapists, counselors, and teachers, who are, after all, professional change agents, also struggle with finding ways to keep momentum going once initial changes are implemented. The relapse rate treating addictions is depressingly high. The likelihood of enduring success in working with many other presenting complaints is also pretty dismal.

Take, as an example, your own experience making simple New Year's resolutions. It is an easy hypothesis to test empirically. Just review the number of times you have resolved to change your life in some significant way, or even just to lose a few pounds or start an exercise program. Now recall the enthusiasm and determination with which you began your change efforts. Maybe you purchased some new "props" to make the job easier—a brand new pair of running shoes, an exercise machine, or a membership in a health club. Certainly you announced to the world your intentions. Alas, before you knew it, your motivation vanished. The wheels of daily routine reduced your change resolutions to faint memories.

Advice from experts (Presbyterian Healthcare Services, 1999; Texas Medical Association, 1999) about how to keep New Year's resolutions appears sound. Get plenty of sleep so as to minimize stressors. Reduce alcohol consumption, which lowers inhibitions. Reward yourself for small measures of success. Remind yourself of the benefits you will enjoy. It is hard to argue with these suggestions. Unfortunately, relying on standard interventions and conventional wisdom is equivalent to facing a ruthless, vicious enemy with a few pebbles to defend yourself. Although they may give you the feeling that you are doing something constructive, ultimately these tools don't do the job nearly as well as needed during such desperate circumstances.

Confusion and Conflict

Every therapist has a fairly well-articulated theory and set of assumptions by which to explain how change takes place. Various schools of thought identify the specific conditions and variables most likely to produce desired changes. It is, of course, fairly confusing that so many of our theories appear to conflict with one another. While some advocates believe passionately that change efforts are best directed toward understanding the past, others concentrate on the present or future. Many clinicians advocate, without the slightest doubt or uncertainty, that change takes place primarily on a cognitive level—through the altering of underlying thought patterns. Others, however, are just as convinced that *real* change can occur only after addressing affective arousal and resolution (accessing and expressing feelings). Still other clinicians believe with all their hearts that all therapeutic interventions take place on a behavioral level.

The debates among various therapists about the best way to promote change are long-standing and apparently impervious to change themselves! Practically every year a new theory appears on the scene that promises to render all others obsolete. Thus practitioners are admonished to abandon their previous attempts to uncover unconscious desires, access unexpressed feelings, dispute irrational beliefs, or realign family power structures and instead to focus their energies on reconstructing different narratives or reprocessing images that occur during eye movements. The fact that we do not really understand how these approaches promote apparent changes seems less bothersome than the doubts of the heathen nonbelievers who persist in using their older, "archaic" methods.

Yet such conflicts are part of the very fabric of change. "Change means movement," declares 1960s radical activist, Saul Alinsky (1971). "Movement means friction. Only in the frictionless vacuum of a nonexistent abstract world can movement or change occur without that abrasive friction of conflict."

To add further to the confusion and conflict is the fact that lasting change is not necessarily related to the length of treatment. What is important, Mahoney (1997) contends, is not how long therapy lasts, but what is done with the time spent together.

Don't Ask

A mistake that therapists sometimes make is to ask an elated client who is rejoicing at recent progress attained what it was that made the most difference. More often than not, the answer is not what would be expected or desired. All too often, therapists hear about something we supposedly did or said that we can't even remember. Worse yet, people often mention some incidental thing that happened, completely unrelated to the intended treatment.

I recall basking in the pride of a client's excessive exuberance over a breakthrough. She was absolutely ecstatic about progress she had recently made. While she was relating the things that would now be different in her life, I was reviewing in my mind which of my many brilliant interventions had made the ultimate difference. I was torn between the poignant metaphor I created the week before and a delayed reaction to my confronting her vigorously a few sessions back. My big mistake was asking her what helped the most.

"It's your shoes," she told me shyly.

"My what?" What the heck was she talking about? I hadn't created a metaphor about shoes.

"Well, it's just...."

"Go on," I urged her, now genuinely curious about some "shoe technique" that I couldn't even remember trying. No matter, I thought; there were lots of things I did in sessions about which I had little recall that still had a big impact. That, I said smugly to myself, is the value of being a veteran therapist. There are literally hundreds of things I do every session, most of them effortlessly and unconsciously, that produce dramatic gains. But I still couldn't remember anything about shoes.

"It's your shoe," she said again pointing at my left foot sporting my favorite pair of loafers. I have very flat feet and these were one of the few pair of shoes that actually felt comfortable.

"Yeah?" I said, looking down to where she was pointing, utterly convinced she was losing her mind.

"You've got a hole at the bottom of your shoe," she said, and looked at me expectantly, as if that explained the dramatic shift in her thinking during the intervening week and all the changes she was now initiating in her life.

"Your point?" I asked, a little more harshly than I intended. I couldn't help it. This was *so* frustrating and not going at all like I had hoped, especially with a client who had just finished telling me how much she had been helped in therapy.

"Well...," she started, then paused, as if embarrassed by what she was going to say. "It's that hole you have on the bottom of your shoe."

I twisted my ankle so that I could see what she was talking about. Sure enough, the leather bottom of my favorite shoes was worn in the center of the sole, showing a rather large hole that I had not really noticed, or if I had, decided to ignore. After all, I would never find another pair of shoes like this again. "Damn!", I was thinking to myself when the client continued.

"It's just that you always seemed so confident and poised to me, like you can see through me and know things that I'll never understand. That's part of my problem, you know...."

"Yes," I said impatiently, interrupting her so that she would explain what the heck she was talking about. I still had no idea what the hole in my shoe had to do with her stunning progress.

"I figured that even though you look like you've got it all together, there you are walking around with a hole in your shoe. Either you didn't know it was there, or didn't care. You probably didn't know that every time you cross your leg—and you do that a lot—your clients have to stare at that hole in your shoe." She looked a little pleased with herself at that point, proud that she knew something that I did not.

I nodded my head noncommittally, or at least with what I hoped was apparent indifference. Inside, I was feeling utterly bewildered.

"So," she continued at a faster pace. "I thought to myself during the last week that if you could walk around with a hole in your shoe, then surely I could accept the small imperfections that I have to live with. I mean, I'd never...."

"Yes?", I said, this time with a touch of anger. She was definitely pushing my button now. Not only was this woman telling me that none of my brilliant change techniques had helped her and it was this stupid hole in my shoe that got her attention, but now she was teasing me for the inattention I gave to my appearance.

I have little recollection about what happened during the rest of the session. One thing, for sure: this lady was clearly feeling and acting differently, and in a remarkably short period of time. Furthermore, the impetus for this change was a serendipitous moment that was completely unplanned and unaccounted for. In a hundred years of supervision sessions, I'd never guess what had helped her. Or what she *said* helped her, I reassured myself repeatedly.

When I had talked about this case to colleagues, they agreed with me that it was obviously threatening for her to admit that something I'd done had been instrumental in her progress. She felt some need to minimize, or even diminish, the power of therapy. "In one sense," a colleague remarked, "she has a need to get some last digs in toward you. She obviously feels some degree of hostility and resentment toward you."

I agreed with this assessment, not because I believed it, but because it let me off the hook. The more I thought about the case, though, the more convinced I became that so often incidental, unintentional, and unplanned events become the impetus for change. In spite of our best efforts, most elaborate treatment plans, and well-executed interventions, there really is no way to know for sure what it is we do that matters most to our clients.

Certainly I created conditions with this client that made it possible for her to have a magic moment of insight. I had worked hard over the preceding weeks to build a solid relationship. She had taken small, incremental steps that made her ready for that transformative event. I knew this all to be true. Yet I felt so humbled by this experience. Too often, just when I think I know what's going on, something like this episode throws me for a loop. I begin to question, all over again, what it is about therapy that is most powerful and influential. My wonder and awe for this wonderful profession I've chosen is reborn all over again. I realize that no matter how long I study this field, no matter how many more decades I practice, I will still never get a handle on what is really going on. Just when I think I've got hold of the thing, I see that I've only grabbed a piece of the tail.

Therapists Have No Monopoly

As much as we may think of ourselves as the grand wizards (or maybe wardens) of change efforts, people have been getting along fine without us for centuries. For every person who makes significant and enduring changes within a therapeutic relationship, there are many others who do it on their own. They grit their teeth and do it the old fashioned way.

Several studies comparing therapy to self-help books, for example, found that the latter could be just as useful as professional therapy for a variety of problems (Gould & Clum, 1993; Scogin, Bynum, Stephens,

& Calhoun, 1990). Furthermore, it doesn't seem to matter whether the books are used in conjunction with a workshop or course or read on their own (Tallman & Bohart, 1999).

Therapists don't have the market cornered on effective helping relationships either because many other service personnel such as hairdressers, bartenders, and taxi drivers are also known to help people make permanent changes in their lives (Kottler, Sexton, & Whiston, 1994). This also doesn't include the impact of teachers, coaches, neighbors, coworkers, and friends.

It is indeed enlightening (and a bit disorienting) to ask people about their most enduring, transformative changes. As often as not, they tell tales of a wayward journey to a foreign place, a serendipitous encounter, or a moment of epiphany that came unannounced. They talk about simply waking up one morning and deciding that they'd had quite enough with the way things were and that from now on everything would be different. Even more remarkable, they were able to stick to their commitments for the rest of their lives.

You need to look only as far as your own life experience to identify personal examples of life-altering decisions that have been enduring. This could involve some critical incident, recovery from a traumatic experience, or a moment of revelation in which you decided to change some part of your behavior or lifestyle.

Spend a moment or two in personal reflection to think about the most important changes you have made in your own life. Think back to all the methods you tried before coming upon the most effective strategy. Then, consider what made all the difference and enabled you to continue your efforts, even in the face of temptations, relapses, and setbacks.

Brief Versus Enduring Changes

Understanding the complex factors that contribute to change in any given case is made more confusing by compelling evidence that almost all current theories of change seem to have some value. I imagine a dozen different readers reacting to the case of "the hole in the shoe" mentioned earlier with a different explanation of what really occurred.

Either I am very flexible, or very fickle and easily swayed, but I can see some merit in a host of different change theories. Furthermore, while there may be evidence that some therapeutic approaches are better for certain presenting complaints, there is no single change strategy that has been found to be consistently better than its competitors. Almost all approaches to therapeutic change currently in use work some of the time with some people in some circumstances.

There are several explanations that might account for this phenomenon. Perhaps all the therapeutic approaches are really doing the same things, even though they have different names for their concepts. Maybe they only *look* different but are really far more alike then they pretend. Another related possibility is that all good therapists, regardless of their espoused theories, do essentially the same things in their sessions: they create solid relationships, capitalize on placebo effects, promote cathartic processes, introduce alternative views of reality, facilitate therapeutic tasks, and encourage constructive risk taking. A third explanation is the most disturbing of all: maybe we do not really understand the underlying complexities of change nearly as well as we think we do (Kottler, 1991).

If there is confusion and controversy surrounding the prevailing conceptions and myths about how change best takes place, then there is even more uncertainty about how to make changes last. Regardless of their preferred theoretical allegiances, few therapists feel daunted by the prospect of helping someone to become less anxious, shy, or depressed, or more assertive and proactive. But then if we were really all that effective, why would so many of our clients return to us (or others) for more treatment?

I do not wish to imply that the therapy and counseling professions are not wonderfully useful and effective. In fact, we know from many studies that the vast majority of our clients, approaching 80% to 90% of the people we see, leave as satisfied customers. The problem we have is not in addressing specific, identified complaints that lend themselves to targeted interventions, but rather in supposedly "curing" long-standing dysfunctional relationship patterns, chronic addictions, and other difficult-to-treat problems that have high relapse rates. Even among those symptoms and problems that do lend themselves to brief and incisive relief, the effects do not always last nearly as long as we (and our clients) prefer.

☐ What Do We Understand So Far?

Instead of continuing to emphasize how mysterious, complex, and confusing the change processes are, or how little we really know about the subject, let's take inventory of what we do know.

Some Very Good Reasons

First of all, it's important to understand why there has been such a scarcity of research on the subject of lasting change. Check any textbook on learning or almost any self-help book on the shelves, and you will see lots of good stuff about how to get change going but precious little on how to *keep* it going. There are several reasons why there has been so little written on the subject.

1. *We don't really understand change, much less why and how it continues.* The process of transformation is so complex and unique for each individual, and involves so many variables, that it seems impossible to get a complete picture of everything involved in the process.

2. *The news is usually depressing.* More than half the time someone does begin a change effort, there is likely to be a relapse. Research on therapy outcomes usually measures change when the person first leaves treatment rather than checking again five years later to see if the effects have lasted.

3. *There is little consensus about how to define "relapse" or "failure."* Is it a natural part of the process to experience setbacks? Maybe this language isn't even appropriate for describing what happens when people go through transformations. What some people describe as a "failure" others conceive as an "opportunity for learning." "Relapse" to some is merely part of the predictable, ongoing process.

4. *It's too expensive and time-consuming to do longitudinal studies.* Researchers need tenure and promotion and it takes two years to get a study into print. It's also hard to stay in touch with people over a lifetime. There are thus very few extrinsic rewards for looking at change over longer periods of time.

5. *Change is not necessarily progressive or incremental, and therefore not easily recognized or measured.* Systems theory, brief therapies, and other recent innovations have demonstrated that change may sometimes take place in sudden spurts. Furthermore, change tends to last when it is supported and reinforced by the larger system to which a person belongs. This includes not only one's family and friends, but also one's physical, social, and cultural environment which may or may not be conducive to maintaining changes. This makes it nearly impossible to identify, much less study, all the variables that might contribute to the process.

6. *It is the nature of the world, both in physical as well as human processes, that things are in a constant state of flux.* Very little holds still long enough for us to grab it, much less make sense of it.

7. *Lasting change is in the eye of the beholder and the objective observer.* Does change last as long as the person believes that it endures?

It is no wonder, then, that there is marked reluctance to talk about lasting change. Outdoor clothing manufacturers like North Face or Helly Hansen may issue lifetime guarantees for their products, but no reasonable therapist or teacher could possibly do the same—nor would that be desirable since change isn't always such a wonderful thing.

In spite of the scarcity of research on the subject, as well as identified impediments, we can draw several general conclusions about what makes change last. Many of these factors are discussed more fully throughout the book.

A Look at the Big Picture

Therapists and counselors are concerned primarily with promoting changes on the scale of an individual life, or perhaps of a family system. When we look at changes that endure over time, we usually take measurements in decade-long intervals. In fact, we are usually darn proud if we have had a hand in producing some positive outcome that has lasted ten or more years.

What if we look at the phenomenon of change over a much longer time period, lasting centuries rather than mere decades? Why is it that some discoveries and inventions are doomed to obscurity while others' influence endures over several generations? We could say that much depends on the quality of the idea or discovery, but we would also be naive to think that political and social forces don't have a huge role in determining what will be remembered and what is forgotten.

In his historical survey of human discovery from the ancient Babylonians to the present, Boorstein (1983) nominated several inventions that have been most significant in contributing to human knowledge. In the order of their appearance, these are:

1. the portable clock and compass which made it possible to take exact navigational readings of longitude
2. the telescope and microscope which opened up the world of science
3. the printing press and movable type which made it possible to disseminate information.

Why does Boorstein consider these inventions more significant than all others? First, because of the *magnitude* of change they made possible. And second, because of their *consequences*—each set in motion so many other changes that followed them.

The object of this lesson in history is to remind us that we are not only interested in the quantity of change, that is, how much and how long, but also its enduring significance in the lives of our clients. It may be quite easy to help clients make small, permanent adjustments in the way they conduct their lives, but if such changes don't really improve the quality of life in a meaningful way, this was not such a successful enterprise. It pays, therefore, to have ambitious goals. This is true even in this era of managed care and brief therapies.

Continuing with an exploration of change on a grand scale, evolutionary theorists and geologists see nothing as permanent. Living beings continue to adapt as the world around them changes, although such changes take place over hundreds of thousands, even millions of years. For example, we consider the ground we stand on and our inborn instincts as about as permanent as things get. Yet, depending on which part of the world you are standing on, things may have looked very different a few decades ago.

In the part of the world that I currently reside as I write these words—Iceland—there are whole islands that did not exist a generation ago. Furthermore, outside of Reykjavik where I am living, there is very little about the earth that is stable and permanent. Because it is situated right on top of the fissure between the North American and European plates, earthquakes are constantly shifting the ground, rearranging the space, growing new mountains, and burying others in glacial ice. Between the violent North Atlantic storms, the bubbling lava, and subsequent melting glacier ice, change in this part of the world is such a constant that people here are used to the earth literally moving underneath their feet. In addition, instead of watching television for entertainment (a hopeless cause anyway because of the lack of English programming), I prefer to watch the weather change outside the window.

Just an hour ago, there was a raging snowstorm with accumulations of several inches. Then the sun came out, accompanied by a warm wind that melted the snow. I quickly put on my running gear and prepared to go out for some exercise when an incredible hailstorm began, raining Styrofoam pellets. Then the real rain started, the horizontal kind that covered the windows in sheets of water so thoroughly that I thought I was on board a ship. And this was all in a single hour!

Moving further into the realm of physical change, there has been a long tradition of philosophers and psychologists looking at the laws of physics and science to understand human behavior. There was a time, in fact, up until the last century or two, when philosophy and science were indistinguishable as disciplines. Sigmund Freud borrowed liberally from his neurological training to describe the complex nature of intrapsychic processes. The earliest concepts of family systems work evolved by Norbert Wiener (1948), Ludwig von Bertalanffy (1968), and Gregory Bateson (1972) used science terms such as "feedback loops," "equilibrium," and "homeostasis" to describe the ways that human organizations resist change in order to maintain stability just like the mechanisms within the human body. According to these models, change endures only when the whole system is restructured to accommodate different environmental conditions (Goldenberg & Goldenberg, 2001).

Looking Smaller Too

When looking at the "bigger picture" of how change endures, or when it fails to last, we can also delve into the subatomic realm of quantum mechanics. Investigating the changes in spin of a top, for example, reveals that energy dissipates itself not in small, incremental steps but in large chunks. "In other words," writes Zukav (1979, p. 207), explaining the process of how momentum runs out, "when a spinning top slows down, its rotation does not diminish smoothly and continuously, but in a series of tiny steps." This occurs so slowly, with steps so close together, that you can't actually see the loss of energy in the top. What was once a smooth motion becomes jerky until all action ceases. If we apply this same model of sustained spin rotation to the behavior of a recovering addict or divorcee, or anyone who is working hard to maintain momentum, we can witness similar progressive deterioration, but only after the top falls.

Of course, there are limits to analogies that compare patterns of human and physical properties. James de Wit, a chemist, reports that "it hardly seems fair to compare a chemical reaction to a human reaction. A chemical reaction either happens or it does not happen. There is nothing in between. When two such chemicals are combined properly, they react; if they are not properly combined, they do not react. Humans are much more complex" (Zukav, 1979, p. 46). Complex yes, but still subject to the physical laws of the universe, especially with regard to the immutable limits to change like gravity and death.

Applying First Aid

So, what does all this have to do with the jobs that we are hired to do? We are often requested to take care of a little problem—a kid who whines excessively, someone who can't sleep or who sleeps too much, a sexual dysfunction, a conflicted relationship, a compulsive or self-destructive behavior. We dutifully assign a diagnosis, plan a treatment, carry forth with the helping effort in the briefest possible period of time, then cross our fingers and hope it sticks. Next in line please.

Day in and day out, week after week, year after year, we see so many people file through our offices. Each believes he or she is a victim of plague, bewitchment, or bad luck. Each is impatient and demands an instant cure, one that comes with lifetime guarantees. In our effort to relieve their pain and appease other interested parties (parents, insurance companies, supervisors), we hurry things along as best we can. We wave a magic wand, speak a few incantations, do whatever we do that is intended to provide help, and then move along to the next case. Our primary concern is to fix things just as fast we can, especially in today's professional climate that no longer values work intended for the long haul. We are like emergency personnel who apply a few bandages, splints, and words of reassurance, and then send people back into battle without much time to consider the bigger picture of the wars they are fighting and why.

A Marathon, Not a Sprint

Despite all we learn in training about helping people to change, our track record isn't so good when we look at the bigger picture of lasting change. If we were completely honest with our clients and told them about their actual prognoses—not in the short-term but over their lifetimes—we would have some very discouraged consumers.

Everyone starts out telling themselves they will be immune from the temptations that strike weaker souls. People willingly invest their life savings into new businesses even though they are aware that 95% of them will fail. Likewise, roughly 80% of people who stop smoking don't maintain their abstinence. Therapy for depression is a relatively effective treatment, with 80–90% recovering to previous functioning levels. Unfortunately, more than half of these people (some estimates as high as 75%) will eventually lose the progress they have made and experience a major relapse (Beck, 1967). This same percentage of relapse rate holds true for many other complaints—anxiety, panic disorder, obsessive compulsive disorder. The prognosis is even worse for addictions.

Young people have unprotected sex with partners who are clearly at risk for carrying deadly diseases, but they tell themselves, "It won't happen to me." Likewise, many who begin a change effort think, "This is it. I'm different from others. I know this will last."

When, Not If

The question is not so much *if* a change effort will fail, but *when* the first relapse will occur. No matter how many books like this one reads, how long a person remains in therapy, how many self-help programs someone subscribes to, or how committed a person feels to taking charge of his or her life, there *will* be setbacks.

Among those who hire a therapist to help them maintain their changes, most relapse within the first year. Thus even with professional assistance, permanent change is an iffy proposition. Whether these relapses become temporary or not depends on how well you prepare for the long run ahead.

In order to be among the relatively few individuals who are successful not only in making needed changes in their lives, but maintaining them, clients must recognize just how formidable a mission this is. It takes more than guts, which help with the initial surge of progress, but also stamina. "You can't go on a diet to lose weight," the client must be told. "You must adopt the sort of lifestyle changes you can maintain for as long as you live. The same is true with any change you are prepared to initiate. This isn't a sprint but a marathon."

Stories of Personal Transformation

I regularly ask people I have just met is to tell me about the most dramatic change they have ever experienced. While they are thinking about that question, I also ask about what they believe made the most difference to them and accounted for their ongoing transformation.

Answers to Some Nosey Questions

The reactions to my questions are almost always predictable. At first, people want to know if I'm really serious about this intrusive question. When they realize that I am sincerely interested, they tend to do one of two things: come closer or run away. For the ones who stick around, I know that the conversation that ensues will be meaningful, intimate, and interesting.

If you think about this question on a personal basis, you are likely to be flooded with images from the past. Many relate to painful times, when you were hurt, lost, rejected, or subjected to ridicule. Others are connected to magical experiences, such as the birth of a child or a new part of yourself. Of the many changes you may have experienced, the one that stands out the most interests me in particular. This is the one that you remember not only because of its magnitude and significance in your life, but also because the effects still last. You are *still* different as a result of what happened.

The logical follow-up question is—What took place that caused you to be so powerfully affected by this experience? In other words, why did the changes last?

I have asked literally thousands of people these questions over the past twenty years. I have made it an assignment in graduate seminars I teach. I have included the questions as part of my intake procedures when I interview a new client. And yes, I also like to ask them of perfect strangers I meet because I know such inquiries will move us to new territory.

☐ Personal Narratives

This chapter investigates stories representative of individuals who have managed not only to change themselves, but also to make the effects persist over time. If we ever hope to become more skilled and effective in promoting these kinds of effects in our clients, we must have a sense of what has worked for others. Most therapists do this routinely but sometimes forget the important follow-up inquiry about how and why the changes endured.

Before getting deeper into the literature and research on change efforts, it seems appropriate to first examine the subject from the perspective of those who have been most successful in their efforts. These stories contain all of the crucial elements discussed in later chapters.

What does it take to quit cocaine, cigarettes, fatty foods, abusive relationships, or impulsive risk-taking? What is required in order for someone to stick with an exercise program? How do some individuals manage to maintain their changes, even in the face of obstacles and temptations?

The narratives that follow should be read with an eye towards identifying those forces and influences that contributed most to the success or failure of the change efforts. Some common issues will be familiar to you in your work with clients, as well as in your own life. These include themes such as taking responsibility for one's life, being forced to grow up, living through physical trauma, redefining oneself, experiencing relationships as instructive, hitting bottom, being stripped of defenses with no place to hide, and going through developmental events and serendipitous moments. In each case, a powerful dimension is illustrated, one that you will wish to attend to in your work with clients, or for that matter, in your own personal change efforts.

Taking Responsibility

When people look back on the changes they have made in their lives learning to be responsible for themselves often stands out as most significant. This often occurs during young adulthood, but throughout our lives we continue to add further episodes that make us more resourceful and confident. Responsibility is learned through many trials and errors, rather than from a single lesson. Nevertheless, there is often a single, momentous incident that stands out above all others.

The first example of permanent changes along these lines is told by a woman, now in her 30s, who remembers an incident that occurred when she was 15 years old, traveling on a school trip to Mexico.

"We were on an overnight train to Mexico City and this was my first experience with alcohol. As I was walking back to the sleeping compartment, the porter tried to molest me in the space between cars. I don't remember feeling scared, just determined that I was going to get out of this situation.

"I made it back to my bed and the creep followed me and kept trying to grope me through the curtains. I woke up my girlfriend and we made a plan that when he tried it again we would grab his hand and I would bite him. Sure enough, he came back another time and I locked onto his wrist and took a huge bite. The next morning I reported the incident to the teacher in charge of our group, but she didn't believe me. When the guy showed up the next morning with a bandaged hand I felt so proud of myself.

"I knew from that experience that I was alone in the world. I would have to take care of myself. If I needed anything out of life, it would be up to me. I also learned how important it was to be supported by others like my friend."

Interestingly, people quite frequently tell such stories of learning to be more resourceful and personally responsible when they were on their own in a strange environment. It almost appears that the more novel the environment, the further away from "home," the more potential there is for getting someone's attention in a significant, lasting way (Kottler, 1997).

A man of about the same age also identifies a time in his early life when he changed the most. He was away from home for the first time on an athletic scholarship to a college far, far away from anything that was familiar.

"Our coach was from the Australian Outback and he was determined to run our sorry, coddled, Texas asses into the ground. He did, and our spirits ended up there too. I was constantly physically abused and verbally harassed and publicly humiliated. On top of that, I wasn't doing well in my classes, I hated my roommate, and the town we lived in sucked. I had no career interests, no social life, and no prospects. I slept constantly to escape, praying that one morning I just wouldn't wake up."

This man felt completely unprepared to handle the situation he now found himself in. He could no longer depend on his parents or friends for support or to bail him out. Somehow, he would have to find the resources to deal with this situation on his own. "Ultimately," he says, "it was my anger that propelled me to do what was needed."

This man was able to overcome his inertia and helplessness by acknowledging his anger as a starting point. "When I am able to get in touch with my anger and sort it out, I find great freedom, creativity, and motivation for change. To get out of my funk, I had to realize how unsatisfied I was living in hell. This was the most important decision I ever made."

Driven by his anger, he developed a plan detailing what he needed to do to escape the unhealthy situation. He jumped on his studies with a vengeance, knowing he had to get his grades up if he was ever going to transfer out of there. Once he began to apply himself to his classes, his grades improved, and his depression lifted.

This incident and the one told by the woman on the train became critical object lessons in these young people's lives. When they speak about these events, they do so with reverence, as if they were initiation rites—which of course they were. In fact, the effects of these changes continue to last until the present day precisely because these individuals have chosen to immortalize them. Whenever they face new struggles, they draw on the strength that they once demonstrated when they first realized they had no one to depend on but themselves.

I have heard stories like this quite a lot, as has any therapist. Clients (and others) frequently report that among their most memorable learning experiences were those in which they learned to assume greater responsibility for their lives as a result of facing adversity on their own. In many forms of therapy we attempt to help people reconnect to such prior successful experiences of being resourceful and then build on them to overcome current struggles.

☐ The Day I Grew Up

Throughout most of my school years, I was stupid. I don't mean that I made dumb mistakes; I mean that almost everyone in my life—my parents, my teachers, my friends—treated me as the marginal student that I was. I could never figure out how to plot sentences grammatically. (To this day I can't tell the difference between a subject and an object, although I know that verbs are "actions words".) In math classes, when I was asked to come to the board and solve a problem, I would just stand there bewildered, staring at the chalky numbers, willing them to reveal their secrets. Thank God there was a family business for me to go into, my parents thought, because I surely wouldn't amount to much. After all, I wasn't the brightest, most athletic, or socially comfortable kid around.

I had difficulty getting into college and only managed to gain entrance into a regular university when the admissions counselor became impressed that I showed up for an interview without my parents. He admitted me on probation. (Interestingly, 15 years later, this counselor ended up as my colleague in the counselor education department of this same university.)

I was tired of being mediocre in everything I did. Most of all, I wanted to be smart. I remember vividly the day I sat outside the dormitory the second semester of my freshman year. It was one of those Michigan spring days when the chill has finally left the air and you can sit outside for hours if you are wearing a sweater and can find a patch of sun. I was sitting on the steps just watching people walk by and making up stories about who they were and what they did. The engineering students were easy to identify because in those days they carried slide rules in little holsters on their belts and had little pocket protectors in their shirts that were filled with brightly colored pencils and pens. It was also easy for me to tell who were the partyers and who were the serious students: the smart kids carried around books, armfuls of them.

In that moment, I had my epiphany. It occurred to me with that single observation that the main difference between smart people and little old average me was that they carried books around, and presumably read them. If I wanted to be smart, all I had to do was the same thing. I didn't wait more than a few minutes before hurrying over to the bookstore to load up on an armful of books that I could carry around with me wherever I went. It wasn't enough to borrow them from the library; I wanted to *own* them so they would become part of me.

That was the day I changed my life. Once I started carrying around books, I pretended that I was smart. The more of the books I actually read, the more smart I started to feel. Then other people started to treat me as if I were smart, asking me for help with things. It was then that I realized I really was smart, and it all started with that day I grew up.

Another common theme we hear in sessions is how powerful transformations can be if the client manages to convince himself or herself that life changes are a matter of deciding to be different and then sticking with that decision. Of course, we can tell people this until we are breathless, and it still won't get through to them until they are open and ready to hear it. The magic and mystery of what we do is how we make this message heard.

Another story that follows this theme is revealed by an English teacher in China who remembers the anguish of being told at age 12 that she couldn't see her father anymore. A number of changes were initiated thereafter that remain until this day.

"Nobody told me anything about where he was, or where he went, or why he wasn't around anymore. He was just gone. My mother seemed to be always hurrying in and out, barely even talking to me, much less explaining anything. I didn't dare to ask any questions since everyone looked so serious. I was afraid of what I might learn. Besides, I was a timid, shy, and introverted girl at that time.

"It wasn't until 4 weeks later that I was told my father was in the hospital and he missed me. The problem was that he was 40 miles away. My 18-year-old sister went to buy some food and asked me to wait for her at the bus station."

"It seemed such a long time to wait that I got on the bus for my first long-distance trip by myself, thinking my sister must have left for the hospital without me. Then I realized that the money I had with me was only half of what was needed for the fare. When I was asked my destination, I gave the driver all my money and lied about where I was going, hoping that she wouldn't notice that I was really going much further. My red face and trembling voice must have told her what I was up to because she challenged me in the most embarrassing way imaginable, calling me a liar. 'I will tell your teacher,' she threatened me in front of all the passengers who stared at me. I wanted to disappear."

"I just sat there and tried to hold back the tears. I kept thinking of my father and how much I missed him, how I could put up with anything if I could just see him. When I found his ward in the hospital, all the tears finally poured out. He looked so sick and pale lying there. He just looked at me but couldn't speak. He couldn't even say my name."

"My father had a cerebral hemorrhage and had been confined to this hospital all this time. I don't know why nobody told me this, but from then on, I went to the hospital by myself every chance I got. Father eventually learned to say some simple words, and gradually learned to walk with my help. He died ten years later, but he was quite content with everything in the family and very proud that I became a college teacher."

"From that first day I visited my father in the hospital, completely on my own, I stopped being a child and became an adult. I knew then that I could not rely on anyone but myself. I would have to take care of myself because I couldn't depend on anyone else. The really amazing thing is that my whole personality changed on that day as well. I was no longer the shy girl anymore. From that time onward, I became open, independent, optimistic, and ready to face all possible challenges."

Like the example of the spinning top mentioned in the preceding chapter, lasting changes often don't follow a pattern of slow, gradual, and incremental shifts in behavior. As illustrated in these examples, change can result from sudden, irrevocable decisions that result from new insights. This, of course, has huge implications for what we do in therapy—that is, if what people report is what actually transpired.

A Slight Digression on the Nature of Truth

I wonder about stories like these, my own as well as those of clients and people I talk to. How much of them are true? Did things really occur the way they are described? Can we actually rely on this data as reasonably accurate descriptions of personal transformation? What if this woman really changed not because of the solitary bus journey, but because of something else she has forgotten, or distorted, or repressed? What if my own story of personal redemption did not occur at all as I remember it? What then can we learn from these lessons?

Therapists have long recognized the difference between "narrative" and "historical" truth (Spense, 1982). Quite early in his research, Sigmund Freud made a distinction between clients' fantasies versus what really occurred. He also noted that it didn't seem to matter whether certain events actually took place as long as people believed they were real. Constructivists, constructionists, phenomenologists (the distinctions sometimes elude me), and other post-modern theorists also share the conviction that reality exists only as a creation in someone's head.

I don't actually believe that all reality is personally constructed. I think it really does matter whether events actually transpired the way they are remembered, more or less anyway. That is why we make some effort to corroborate client stories, to check their histories, and to look for inconsistencies in their narratives. People who lie to others are often lying to themselves, and what we stand for above all else is the seeking of truth (whatever that is).

The tricky part, of course, is determining what is real. I am utterly convinced, beyond the slightest doubt, that I became smart on that spring day outside my residence hall. That is the way I remember it, so that is the way it was. You can't convince me otherwise. Well, actually you could, if you had some evidence.

My brother once revealed to me on the phone that he had recently "discovered" in therapy the source of his life-long problems with intimacy. "It was when you moved out of the house," he accused me, "that you left me alone to take care of Mom." He was referring to the time when I moved in with my father to escape my alcoholic, depressed mother, leaving him to take care of our mother and younger brother.

"Ever since I was 10 years old, I had to take care of things at home. My therapist explained all this to me," he said with relief in his voice, as if this provided the long-lost answer he had been searching for.

I hesitated whether to say anything, but finally couldn't resist. "There is only one problem with that theory though."

"It's not a theory!" he protested. "That is what really happened."

"Well, you are right about one thing," I deadpanned.

"Yeah?" he answered suspiciously.

"I did move out of the house like you told your therapist."

"Right." I could hear the relief in his voice, but also some hesitance as if he could feel the other shoe about to drop.

"The only problem," I told him, "is that you weren't 10 when I moved out. You were 14. I was actually there, in the house, the whole time. I was the one who had to call her psychiatrist when she threatened to kill herself. I was the one..."

My brother hung up.

We laugh about this now, but it illustrates the ways that therapists sometimes contribute to the fictions people use to order their chaotic lives. Maybe, ultimately, it doesn't matter that much whether the stories are completely accurate portrayals of what happened. Not only is there no way to know for sure, but to a certain extent, what we believe happened does present a kind of reality that we live in.

Serious Like a Heart Attack

The expression, "serious like a heart attack," has particular poignancy for Nate who was swimming one day when he felt a shortness of breath. He went to sit down in a chair by the pool when he felt himself lose all energy, as if he were paralyzed. The next thing he knew, Nate was on his way to the hospital in an ambulance.

"The emergency room offered more opportunities to distract myself from my growing fear. It was a busy place, brightly lighted. One doctor, who was talking on the phone to a surgeon, began describing a patient who had evidence of acute anterior-wall myocardial infarction. I wondered who he was talking about until I realized it was me! I felt so helpless and out of control."

Everything had changed in Nate's life with the betrayal of his body. He began to slip into a deep depression. "I was shocked to feel completely out of breath after merely stepping out of bed. I could only walk a few steps without resting. Parts of me felt numb. Every time I moved, I lived in terror that it would spark another heart attack."

Nate was a young man, only in his early forties, yet now he felt like everything in his life was different. This confrontation with his own mortality got his attention as nothing else had previously.

Time after time, people who recover from life-threatening events, whether sparked within their own bodies or by some natural disaster, report that these events changed them forever, for better or worse. The saying that what doesn't kill you makes you stronger is not really true; it can also make you much weaker.

I heard the stories of two men, brothers-in-law about the same age. Both men worked as fishermen and lived in a small village of a few hundred people in the West Fjords of Iceland. When a terrible avalanche buried their village one night, these two men became involved in the rescue of their families and neighbors. All the next day, they pulled out the frozen, bent bodies of their loved ones, sobbing and crying all the time they worked. That day will live in the minds of both individuals as a permanent transformative event. They were changed forever.

What is interesting, however (and we have witnesses this time), is that each of them chose to react to the disaster in a different way. One man's life virtually ended that day and he has never (as yet) recovered from the trauma. He is dead on his feet, barely moving through his life. The other man, however, decided that he would do a whole lot of things differently after that day. He became more alive.

The job of a therapist is to help people make new, more useful interpretations of their tragedies and disappointments. We are the ones charged with helping people to create meaning out of their life experiences, to recover from setbacks by choosing more desirable interpretations of what transpired. Whether framed in the language of the cognitive, narrative, constructivist, humanist, or reality therapist, our job is to help people see their heart attacks or avalanches as opportunities for growth rather than signals of their impending demise.

☐ This Is Who I Am

"It all started out with a friend of mine who lost 40 pounds." Jonathon is telling the story of how he made new behaviors habitual, and he is trying hard to restrain a smile lest he appear too proud of himself. "He's a guy about my age and we are a lot alike, so I thought if he could do it, so could I."

Jonathon has been struggling to lose weight, and keep it off, during most of the last decade. He was about to give up and accept himself as a fat, aging man when his friend's success modeled the behavior that he so craved for himself. It showed him what was possible and within reach.

"It wasn't like this one incident did it for me. I'd been thinking about being trim for a long time. But this is kind of what pushed me over the edge."

I was nodding my head in agreement as I listened to him. He seemed so proud of himself and what he had been able to accomplish. But I wasn't nearly as impressed as I pretended to be. I've seen so many people lose weight, sometimes the same 40 pounds over and over again. What really struck me, though, was that it had now been over 3 months and Jonathon hadn't gained back a single pound. Even more impressive to me is that he went off the diet he had been on—eating meat and eggs—and was now just following a sensible eating plan.

"I eat everything now," he said, "just in reasonable portions."

Jonathon kept wanting to tell me about how he lost the weight but I know enough stories about how to change. Instead, I kept redirecting the conversation to how he had been able to stick with his plan.

"I have a different mindset now. This is who I am. Once you get into a routine like this, it's easy."

That statement seemed so profound, so accurate in describing what made it possible for him to redefine himself as a nonfat person. He made the new behaviors habitual. The change became permanent because it was no longer negotiable.

Just a month earlier, Jonathon experienced a critical point in his efforts to maintain his new weight. "I was on vacation and I gained a pound a day. Once I was back home, though, I have total control over my environment. I learned that I need to have complete control over the structure of my life."

"Why didn't you give up?" I asked him. "You worked so hard, lost all that weight, and then gained so much back in a single week."

"It just felt so good to be on track. I got so many positive affirmations for looking good and I didn't want to give that up."

"So," I challenged him a little, "you did this mostly for others' approval."

"No," he replied thoughtfully. "This big old fat me wasn't me any more."

Another tale of significant weight loss is told by a young woman in her 20s who also managed to change her body image through a critical incident. It all started when she was 16 and decided she was sick of seeing the chubby person staring back at her from the mirror.

"Every day before I went out to play volleyball at school, I would look at myself in the mirror to see if my legs were decent enough to wear shorts. The answer I found was always negative. I felt miserable about what I felt was my greatest shortcoming—a lack of self control."

"About this time, I became infatuated with a pale, old-fashioned, male teacher who I thought was so handsome and charming. I had this love affair with him in my imagination and this stimulated me to make myself look as good for him as I could."

This story could make any feminist cringe, especially the part about her self-esteem and personal worth being directly related to her slimness. Ideas like this often lead to eating disorders. Indeed, this woman went on a crash diet, eating one loaf of steamed bread a day in order to reach her goal. One factor to keep in mind is that this young woman is Chinese, living in a traditional culture that has emphasized her value in terms of attractiveness to men.

This woman had been unhappy as long as she can remember throughout her childhood, although she traces her recovery to the day she decided she had had enough being the fat girl. What she was looking for most was a sense of personal security, one in which her body, as well as her home, felt comfortable to her.

"I think there is one thing which has never changed and will stay there forever in my life—that is my hunger for a safe and warm home. My childhood was not the best experience. I was raised by my mother who was bad-tempered and vented her anger towards the hardness of life by beating her children. When I was small and did not understand my own unhappiness, I tried to find friendship in others, leaving myself mostly dissatisfied."

As you would suspect, although this woman has managed to keep herself slim and trim, this enduring change in body shape has not produced the happiness that she has so longed for.

"Although I am grown now, I still feel eager to find love with a boyfriend or husband. I keep choosing men who are much older than me and who can take good care of me. The differences between us often lead to quarrels. Men have told me that I am too demanding, but I think it is because they are not willing to give enough in the relationship."

So there is a core of valuing herself after all! This woman has been able to maintain her "first-order" change, the reshaping of her physical body, but she still has a way to go with the second- and third-order changes, those that are at the core of her unhappiness and dissatisfaction.

In both of these tales of permanent weight loss, the real test was in the recovery from lapses. The problem is rarely a matter of losing weight, but rather of keeping it off. When faced with a lapse in which they reverted back to old patterns, the fear of returning back to where they had once been was so great, that they were able to recover through sheer force of will. There was no special technique that either one of them used.

I am reminded by these two stories that it doesn't matter nearly as much as people think how they go about initiating their desired changes. What matters most is the extent of their commitment to keeping the momentum going when (not if) they have setbacks.

Learning From Love and Lack Thereof

So many of the myths, stories, novels, movies, and songs in human culture deal with love—searching for it, finding it, losing it, mourning it, healing from it, reveling in it, and seeking fulfillment, joy, and satisfaction through it. Love is not only what people hunger for most in their lives, but is also the vehicle by which life-long changes take place. Who among us cannot remember some lesson, never forgotten, that was learned through the sharing (or desolution) of love?

Most learning about trust, intimacy, companionship, sexuality, rejection, and giving takes place in love relationships—those that are beginning, those that are ending, and most of all, those that endure over time. Some of our clients never seem to learn from past mistakes in such an arena: they pick one loser after another; they seek out lovers who abuse or neglect them; they "teach" partners to treat them disrespectfully; they keep loved ones at a distance or drive them away; and they make themselves as unlovable as they possibly can. And they carry these patterns into their relationships with therapists as well.

What was your first love affair like? When were you hurt worse than you thought you could tolerate? What was the most magical time you ever experienced in your life? When were you driven to distraction? So often, the answers people immediately supply are instances when they were seriously involved, or thought they were, with someone. It is the act of negotiating a mutually comfortable distance, or splitting apart, that leaves its' mark indelibly on one's character. Few experiences are ever more memorable and influential; few have as enduring effects, for better and worse.

The changes that occur in love relationships can be short-acting or permanent. One woman thinks of the time when she broke up with her boyfriend.

"I finally realized that he didn't love me. I think he loved me as much as he could, but it wasn't nearly enough for me. It hurt so much to break things off that I told him on the phone so I wouldn't have to face him.

Afterwards, I cried almost every night while talking to the old memory of him."

"It was after more than a year that I began to feel much better. During this period of recovery, I refused to get involved in any new relationship. When my friends wanted to introduce someone to me, I would try my best to avoid the situation. I might have missed some good men. Who knows? Sometimes I even think it a good idea to remain single the rest of my life."

This woman views this experience as the type of change that didn't last that long. Once she fully recovered, she was prepared to give love another chance. Next time, she wanted to make a better choice, so perhaps she did take something permanent from the previous relationship after all.

"The door to my heart had been tightly shut until I got to know the man I am currently involved with. We first met each other about four months ago. We started out as friends. It was through talking to him, listening to his stories, including a sad love story, that I found myself grow fond of him. But almost immediately I realized that I had to stop liking him. It is said that if a man keeps talking about his former girlfriend, it means he is not yet ready to accept a new one. This is exactly the situation he is in now. Therefore, I have made up my mind to taste the tears alone and bury my feeling at the bottom of my heart, so that I may face him calmly and continue to be friends as usual."

She sees the second relationship as a better teacher than the first one, because now she can make better decisions about how much of herself she is willing to risk. Yet rather than offering a forced choice, relationships seem to offer a continuum of learning experiences. Those lessons that last are the ones that reach us at our core in a way that we are shaken. Once things settle back into place, which can take years, we are left different people.

In therapy, we often attempt to create the kind of idealized relationships in which clients feel honored, respected, and loved, but also challenged. We sometimes use the therapeutic alliance as leverage to promote changes that could not otherwise occur. The hard part, naturally, is to figure out ways for the lessons learned to become indelible so that clients are able to follow the templates that were formed in sessions. Without ongoing support, once the therapeutic relationship ends, clients all too often slip backward.

Sabotage

"People won't let me change," Morgan said with a straight face. Because Morgan is a professional poker player, when he decides to mask what he's feeling, there is no way to read what's going on inside.

For the past few minutes he has been talking about his frustration and anger toward family and friends who keep sabotaging his attempts to soften his demeanor. I look at him encouragingly, nodding my head for him to continue.

"I started telling folks about feeling depressed lately, and not just because I'm losing at the tables." He stops for a minute, smiles to himself, then explains, "Actually, I've been losing *because* I'm depressed."

"So," I interpret, "you're punishing yourself by giving your money away." I am hoping that we can pursue this further. I hold my breath, knowing how rare it is that he ever talks about things that are deeply personal.

Morgan nods thoughtfully. "Yeah, I guess that's it. I almost never drink when I play—although I'm the second best drunk poker player in the world—but I started on double scotches and then just kept going all night."

I'm not sure where this is going, so I try to redirect him back to his earlier comment. "You mentioned before that people won't *let* you change. I'm curious what you mean by that."

He stares at me, or rather through me, as if deciding which card to play next. I now know what it must feel like to sit opposite him at the poker table. I feel transparent even though I am doing my best to keep a straight face.

"It's like this," he says, finally deciding to be frank, "everyone counts on me to be strong, dependable, objective." Tears start to form in his eyes as his voice becomes softer. "I'm a gambler for Christ's sake!" he says in a hoarse whisper. "They all think of me as a machine—always calm, always unflustered."

I nod my head in agreement. This is *exactly* how I see him as well, so I am shocked by this passionate display of feeling.

"So," he continues, "when I admitted to people close to me that I've been feeling down lately, they jumped all over me." He shakes his head as if he can't believe the betrayal.

I am wondering who "they" is, but more to the point, I want to know more about what happened so recently to open his wounds. "Morgan," I prod him gently, "what happened exactly?"

He wipes his eyes, although I can still see moisture pooling on the lower lids. I am fascinated by how skillfully he can keep the tears from falling. I wonder what it would take for him to really let go and let them fall of their own accord.

"I want to be a man who can talk about his feelings, tell people what's going on inside."

"Like you do with me."

"Yeah," he says with relief, "like with you." He looks at me directly and—it was either the upward movement of his eyes or a conscious decision—he lets go and a wet trail snakes down both cheeks. "I don't like being a poker player—hiding my emotions, being manipulative, taking advantage of weakness. I've learned to do this in all my relationships, not just when I'm playing. Yet lately, when I've tried to show a softer side of myself, people don't like it. They want the old me back, the one they are used to."

Morgan is describing a common occurrence that takes place during change efforts. We know from systems analysis and interactive dynamics that when one person's changes disrupts established interaction patterns, everyone else must make necessary adjustments to restore equilibrium. Morgan's family and friends may say that they want him to be more expressive and vulnerable with them, but the reality is that they are quite uncomfortable with this foreign being. They don't know how to respond. They feel disoriented. Most of all, whatever characteristic role he has played in their lives, there is now a vacancy that yearns for a new occupant. When given a choice between making changes themselves to accommodate Morgan's transformation and getting him to resume his previous accustomed role, it is far easier to sabotage the new changes that are initiated.

Change, therefore, doesn't come without a certain degree of resistance—not only from the individual undergoing the often painful transition—but from others who are frightened, confused, and uncomfortable with this novel behavior. I recall another illustrative case with a couple I was seeing in which the husband repeatedly berated his wife for being overweight and sexually unattractive. Yet once she began a determined diet, the husband went out and bought potato chips, chocolate chip cookies, and other tempting treats that he previously never favored. Furthermore, he placed them strategically around the house so that his wife couldn't fail to be within arm's length of them.

When I confronted the man with his puzzling behavior, especially in light of all he had said about wanting his wife thin, he protested innocently, "So, I'm supposed to deprive myself just because *she* has a problem?"

I didn't know whether to slug him or laugh outright. This was the most obvious attempt to sabotage a change effort that I had ever seen. Not only did the husband claim to be oblivious to what he was doing, but the wife also seemed not to realize what he was doing. She just assumed that any weight loss effort on her part was doomed. Indeed it was—as long as the person she lived with was doing his mighty best to make sure she didn't succeed.

Support from a therapist is extremely important to promote lasting changes, but not nearly as critical as encouragement from those the client lives and works with. Unless efforts are made to enhance lifestyle and daily interactions, it is highly unlikely that any changes will be maintained. This is especially the case when one or more significant others is actively involved in sabotage.

Defining Moments

Another phenomenon that we see quite commonly in our most successful cases is a critical incident that get the person's attention in a way that nothing could previously. It is pretty difficult to manufacture such a defining moment in a session, at least in a way that the effects last, although we often attempt to do just that in a number of ways. We want the client to have an "aha" experience, one in which the whole world looks different afterwards.

More frequently, clients bring incidents that could conceivably qualify as defining moments, that is, if we can help them to interpret them as such. Again, the tricky part is encouraging the insight to stick in such a way that new, permanent behavior results.

In this next story, a woman comes face-to-face with an aspect of her lifestyle she despises so much that she can no longer live with herself the way she is. This moment of insight is rarely enough, as she points out, unless there is ongoing support to continue what is learned.

"After 20 years as a high-powered hospital executive, I walked away from my job and didn't look back. This decision all began for me one day when I was on vacation with my family in Hilton Head Island. My daughters were doing their homework as the school year was still underway. They were in second grade at the time."

"I was quite busy, even on vacation, constantly taking hour-long phone calls and doing briefcases full of work. Though I complained about the burden, I was exhilarated by the power and prestige and money that came with it all."

"As they were quietly doing their homework, I walked over to my daughters and hugged first one and then the other. As I hugged the second, I saw she had tears coming down her cheeks. I asked what was wrong and she told me that she thought she was going to fail second grade. I was stunned to hear this because both girls had always done so well in school. I questioned her and learned she was terrified of her teacher the entire school year, and I had not the first bit of an idea that this had been going on in her life."

"That was a defining moment for me, but it was not yet the point at which I acted decisively. After we went home, I met with the teacher and did my best to help my little girl salvage the school year. About a month later, I was getting ready for my long day at the office and I looked at my husband and said, 'This is the worst part of the day.' "

"He asked me what I meant so I told him, 'The whole day is ahead of me.' At that very moment we decided I would leave that job, even though I had nothing else lined up. As I look back on this, I see that what contributed the most to making the change occur was the sadness I felt over my daughter's plight and my lack of awareness, and the thing that made the change last was the support of my husband when he said, 'You have already done more than your fair share.' This wasn't really the case, at least in terms of income generated, but I appreciated the support. In general, I think that support from others is essential to making changes last."

This woman attributes most of her continuing success in maintaining changes to the support she felt from her husband and others. While this is assuredly an important point, there are some other factors evident in her story. For instance, she talks about the incredible sadness she felt toward her daughter's plight. This definitely got her attention in a way that nothing else had up to that point. She doesn't mention a host of other strong emotions that were certainly present—especially guilt over what she then perceived as her parental neglect.

Defining moments such as these seem to exert the most lingering effects when they are accompanied by rather strong emotional activation (Greenberg, Rice, & Elliott, 1993; Greenberg & Safran, 1987; Johnson, 1996). In other words, being really, really upset, makes one ripe for lasting change, provided the experience is processed in a constructive way.

Hitting Bottom

It is not unusual for therapists who work with addictions and impulse disorders to watch clients bounce back and forth between relative stability and continued indulgence in their self-destructive behaviors. In spite of these clients' best intentions and most concerted efforts, once they return to their usual environment, relapse seems inevitable. But when someone runs out of options, when it is perceived that there is really no other choice left, a new leverage becomes available that can be used to not only promote change, but keep it going afterwards.

"The layer of soot over the garage window diffused the sunlight that hit the dirty floor. It was frigid outside, and the garage doors were closed. Earlier I had gotten high and had placed my stash in the wall behind the sink. My cubbyhole was pretty well protected behind a layer of insulation and only accessible by reaching through the fiberglass into the wall. I was pretty sure that nobody would find my drugs."

"This guy who worked for my parents was a crackhead. I didn't trust him and he knew I was high that morning. He had been fucking with me, giving me that knowing smile. Now I was pressing my face against the wall as I reached into my private burrow. As I retracted my hand with what was no longer a prize, but a filthy burden, I stopped. In that single moment, I felt all the emptiness and loneliness of my life. I held the foil wrapped treasure in my hand and started to feel sick. I pulled my knees up to my chest, leaned against the wall, and wanted to cry. But I couldn't. I thought about the rusty screw laying on the floor. I picked it up and traced a faint line across my wrist. I couldn't do that either. What was stopping me?"

"I am better than this, I thought."

When this addict hit bottom, it was as if he couldn't get any worse. He felt such despair that he couldn't even cry for himself. But he realized on the dirty floor of the garage that he deserved better than the life he had created for himself.

"I tried to get a high a few times more," he says, "but nothing happened. No high. I just felt depressed."

It has been 10 years since the day he decided to stop being an addict and he has been able to maintain the change by reminding himself about just how desperate he once felt. "I know that if I want to live I can't do drugs."

When he says "know" he isn't talking about the word in just the cognitive sense, but deep in his heart. He doesn't have the slightest doubt that he would be dead if he didn't stop using drugs when he did. Consistent with the philosophy of "12-step" programs, including Narcotics Anonymous, he thinks of himself as always an addict. He might have appeared to change on the outside by altering his drug-using behavior but nothing has fundamentally changed on the inside where he still feels like an addict. This reminder helps him to still fear a relapse.

This is another common theme among the stories. Those who have been able to maintain their continued progress do so out of not only desire for where they are headed but also intense fear that they might return to where they have been.

No Place to Hide

Candy stayed in her marriage long past the point where it was doing her any good. She deluded herself that things were far better than they really were, mostly because she didn't depend on her husband for anything. After surviving a car wreck that left her housebound for months, Candy finally realized that her husband had never really been there for her. Even at this low point in her life, when she was completely incapacitated, her husband did virtually nothing to help her.

After spending 4 months hobbling around on her own, Candy says, "I had to face the truth about my marriage." "I could no longer delude myself into believing that I was really safer with him than without him. I couldn't soothe myself with the thought that if I was ever hurt and really needed his help, he would do whatever was necessary because he loved me. I filed for divorce and knew I couldn't ever go back. I just couldn't ignore the situation any longer."

I asked her to look back on the experience and identify what made the biggest difference to her. What was it that forced her to make the change—and sustained her when she wanted to change her mind?

"I can't say that it was the wreck alone that made the difference. It was a combination of things. The accident certainly got my attention. I was in a support group immediately afterwards and those relationships were helpful in talking about my feelings. I started paying close attention to the way my husband acted after that. I saw him clearly for the first time. I realize now that my marriage had been bad for a very long time, but I couldn't accept that. Once I was honest with myself, I found the courage I needed. I couldn't lie to myself any more."

Once you've seen the truth, Candy says, you can't pretend you haven't seen it. You can't go back, even if you want to. You can't deny the reality that you have been ignoring, or hiding from.

Another aspect of this narrative is interesting to revisit. When people supply reasons to account for their changes, we have to remember that this may not be what really happened. We tend to distort things a lot when we tell stories, not because we are lying, but because our memories are imperfect. With each telling of the tale, the details may become distorted or embellished. Even if someone does recollect what happened accurately, what he or she identifies as causes may not have been important after all. Candy, for example, believes that it was the car wreck and subsequent reality testing that got her out of the marriage. But what if it had been a succession of incidents that led to the final decision, rather than the simple explanation of one traumatic incident? Or what if her husband dumped *her*?

Our job of figuring out what sustains change is made more complex when we can't rely totally on clients' own explanations for what happened. And in spite of what some might say, it does matter greatly that we operate on reasonably accurate data when trying to make predictions.

It does, however, seem reasonable to assume that when we are forced to face the truth, even if it was provoked by something other than what we believe occurred, we still can't go back. In a sense, we are ruined and must start over again.

Being Forced to Change

Certainly, people can be changed irrevocably against their will. John Watson, B. F. Skinner, and company demonstrated long ago that people can be conditioned to behave in certain ways, or fear certain things, without either their consent or even awareness of what is going on. Nevertheless, to many people, it is the act of choosing their own destiny that makes the changes last once they do realize what has occurred.

A Chinese graduate student describes two very different change experiences, the first thrust upon her without her consent, the second made quite intentionally.

"I was forced to receive military training for a whole year in a province far from my home. During that year, I was trained to obey rules, learn Marxism, and most importantly, to be patient with endless boring lectures from officials. I was very obedient, quiet, and cooperative, at least on the outside. On the inside, however, I resisted everything they tried to teach me. They wanted me to give up acting on my own, so I followed their orders and pretended to accept what they taught. I was not the only one who pretended to change. Once that year was over, the effects did not last long at all, and I returned to the way I was before. Perhaps what I learned the most is that I do not like others nagging me and telling me what to do."

She contrasts this experience in the military with one in which she returned to academic life at Peking University where freedom was valued most. It was her choice to do this; no one pressured her or tried to control her.

"Now I am encouraged to think and act on my own. Rather than following orders or fashions, I have learned to think for myself. This will stick with me as long as I live. I have learned to be myself, rather than someone whom others are trying to shape according to their own molds."

The lesson evident in this woman's experience is an integral part of most helping efforts. The client must be recruited as a partner in the process and must believe that the changes being undertaken are for his or her own good, rather than merely to please others. Often we don't discover that approval seeking was the main motive until there has been a major relapse and clients admit that a huge part of their drive was related to getting someone off their backs.

You Can't Go Back Again

Permanent transformations sometimes take place because of corresponding changes in the body or developmental functioning. There is nothing like facing the aging process, mortality, sickness, disease, or natural developmental processes to get one's attention in a way that can't be ignored.

Upon becoming pregnant, Nancy was ecstatic; it was what she had always wanted. Both she and her husband had planned carefully for their family. They were on a solid financial footing, settled in their careers, and enjoying a very stable, loving relationship.

As is so often the case with pregnancy, everyone responded to Nancy by talking about how wonderful and lucky she was. She positively glowed, she was told over and over. "You must be so happy."

"Miserable does not even begin to describe how I felt," she confides. "I was angry, fat, impatient, and sometimes just plain mean. I had gained about 40 pounds and did not like the way I looked at all. I had always been a size 2 and now, after what seemed like overnight, I became a size jumbo."

To make matters worse, Nancy couldn't talk about her negative feelings to anyone. When you're pregnant, you're supposed to be happy.

"People would say to me, 'Oh, but the baby is worth it.' Clearly, they didn't understand what I was going through. I also started to feel panic at the idea of being responsible for another person. I would be in charge of this tiny, helpless person who would be completely dependent on me. I was terrified."

So far, we have all the elements one needs for a major personal transformation. Nancy was highly aroused emotionally. She felt very out of balance—not just physically but also psychologically. She was desperate to regain her equilibrium. She was thus extremely motivated to do whatever she could to adjust to a situation that made her feel out of control.

"When my son was born, my world flipped inside out and upside down. My husband was affected too, of course, but not nearly as much. He is much more relaxed than I am about all this. Every little peep or cry from my son sends me running to check on him. Is he breathing? Is he wet or dirty? Is he hot or cold? He can't talk so I don't always know what he wants. Yet this utterly strange idea of interpreting his cries has now become second nature to me."

There is now a glow to Nancy's face as she talks about what it means to her to be a mother. She has slimmed down and regained her figure. She appears confident in her new role, with most of her doubts addressed. She looks back on the person she used to be, just a few months ago, and is blown away by the changes. "I am changing every day because of this little person who has not yet said one word to me."

Nancy's world has been turned upside down due to a developmental transition. Once you have passed the point of no return, with the birth of a child, the beginning or end of a marriage, the death of a loved one, even the passage of a milestone birthday, you can't ever go back. You are stuck in a new world.

In a sense, we try to help clients recreate their situations so they can't go back again to where they were. We help them to burn bridges that cross back into mediocrity or misery. We try to restructure things so that even if they wanted to revert back to previous dysfunctional patterns, they wouldn't be permitted to do so.

We "ruin" clients in a variety of clever ways. Sometimes a powerful insight is enough, fostering some revelation about the way a client is playing games or bringing the "secondary gains" of dysfunctional behavior more clearly into focus. Another strategy is to encourage clients to confront antagonists or take irrevocable steps that cannot be undone. Once clients realize they have no choice except to go forward and that there is no option for going backward, it is a lot easier for them to maintain the changes.

Serendipity

So often, the changes we undergo are not necessarily those we seek. We may be minding our own business, going about the daily affairs of our lives, when WHAM, out of nowhere fate intervenes. We don't ask for these encounters; if we had a choice in the matter, most of the time we would decline the opportunity. Nevertheless, sometimes we walk through an open door and are forever changed.

One such door in the life of Sandy was hanging on a rusted van heading west down the interstate. "I was hitchhiking on the highway when this family stopped to pick me up. I was 19 at the time, in search of my next adventure. They invited me into their world, so I lived with them on their houseboat. I learned things I never thought possible. I changed my eating habits. I learned about sewing my clothes, making sculpture, taking care of kids. I was in such an impressionable stage, and I was so open to everything they offered."

What if this couple had not stopped to pick her up?, Sandy wonders. She would be such a different person today. Yet now she meets so many people who are just as interesting and influential, but they don't have nearly the same impact. What made the difference to her at the time was how open she was to new experiences, a condition that seems to dissipate with age.

Serendipitous events can change us only if we are open and ready for what they offer. That is one reason why change happens more easily when we are traveling. During trips our eyes and ears and senses are much more open. We make ourselves more accessible. We become much more aware of things around us and more willing to experiment and take risks.

Therapy is a journey of sorts, a trip into the unknown in which the rules are different from those of everyday life. We help clients open themselves up to new possibilities and opportunities, not by actually creating more adventures, but by helping them to view their lives that way.

The Two-Minute University

The journey of growing to be a better counselor or therapist is one that is most often chosen freely. You are reading this because you want to learn more about the way changes last. Nobody is forcing you to study this subject, even if this book is an assignment in a required class. At any time, you can choose not to attend. Like the Chinese student, you can pretend to change. You can say the right things and act as your teacher wants you to act. But inside you can remain exactly the same, if that is your choice.

Will this book have a lasting effect on you, or will it just gather dust on your shelves with all the others you have read, collected, and then forgotten about? Will you sell it back to the bookstore so that no reminder is left?

One of the characters from old *Saturday Night Live* episodes was Father Sarducci, a comic dressed as a priest from the Vatican who spoke in a thick Italian accent. One of his routines was something he called the "Two-Minute University" in which he promised to teach in a few minutes everything that the average person would remember from university classes about ten years after graduating.

"For instance," he would say, "take Economics. What do you remember about this subject now? At the Two-Minute University, it takes only a few seconds to teach you everything about economics that you would actually remember from a traditional class several years after you graduated."

"Are you ready?" Father Sarducci would say in his thick accent, preparing the audience to pay attention. "Okay. This is it. Supply and demand. That's all you need to know about Economics. Okay. Now let's move on to Spanish...."

This is very funny, but also quite true. We really do remember so little from any class we take, any workshop we attend, or any book like this that we read. Retention is even more dismal when others make us study or read something that we don't find relevant or personally important. That is one reason why I am introducing this subject first through the stories of people who have made permanent changes. If these narratives captivate and interest you, then perhaps you will stick around long enough to hear the rest. Certainly they sensitize you to look for the common themes that have occurred in your own experiences, as well as in those of your clients.

Kinds of Change: Magnitude, Rate, Levels, and Significance

Nothing lasts forever. Even granite is ground to sand after a few million years. Permanence is not only impossible, but in the case of humans, it is hardly adaptive. According to what we know about evolution, natural selection favors those who are most flexible and amenable to change. Although constant adaptation might be advantageous to a species over the course of its evolution, relative stability is often useful for individuals within a single lifetime.

There isn't a strict parallel between change among living things and change in the physical world. Animals alone have a metabolism that transforms energy in such a way that they can move freely about (Curtis, 1991), although it has been said that water invented humans merely as a way to transport itself from one place to another (Robbins, 1976).

Although change is such a familiar part of life, it is not necessarily a state with which we ever grow comfortable. "Most of us are about as eager to be changed," writes novelist James Baldwin (1977), "as we were to be born, and we go through our changes in a similar state of shock."

Definitions of What Lasts

Before we delve too deeply into the subject of change, it is important to define our terms. This is not as easy as it sounds because it is fairly challenging to determine when a shift is truly permanent.

When I speak of lasting change, I'm not referring to "forever" but rather to change that has these components:

1. It is internalized. The change becomes a part of the person rather than a temporary aid that the person holds outside of himself or herself.
2. It is significant or transformative. We are not talking about a small, inconsequential alteration but a major shift in perception and behavior.
3. It results not only in altered thinking and feeling but also in altered behavior. All facets of human experience are affected and impacted by the change.
4. The change remains stable until such point that it is no longer adaptive.

Change is often defined as a relatively permanent process; if effects don't last, then it couldn't have made much of an impact. Nevertheless, there are some very different conceptions about what change involves—whether it is essentially a cognitive, attitudinal, behavioral, affective, or biological process. Some theorists, beginning with Greek philosopher Parmenides, contend that all change is but an illusion; reality is a permanent, unalterable condition.

In her novel *Breathing Lessons*, Anne Tyler's character is ruminating about whether to marry or not, skeptical that anything in her life would be different (1988).

"There was no such thing ... as real change. You could change husbands, but not the situation. You could change *who*, but not *what*. We're all just spinning here, she thought, and she pictured the world as a little blue teacup, revolving like those rides at Kiddie Land where everyone is pinned in his place by centrifugal force."

This might sound like a strange point of view in light of our contemporary post-modern, constructivist beliefs that reality is so changeable that it has no fixed state at all. Thus, reality is whatever you want it to be, or at least whatever you think it is.

Structural Changes

It was Kuhn (1962) who so eloquently observed that changes can either take place within existing paradigms, or lead to shifts in the frameworks themselves. Change on a structural level is thus a "second-order" alteration, which is differentiated from a "first order" change (Becvar & Becvar, 1988; Lyddon, 1990; Watzlawick, Weakland, & Fisch, 1974). The latter represents a "little," incremental change that appears on the surface. This is a linear, simple adjustment. Second-order change is far more significant in magnitude, deeper in penetration to the core, with effects that are longer lasting. It involves a "radical restructuring of a person's core self, mode of being, or worldview" (Hanna & Ritchie, 1995, p. 176).

In the practice of therapy, obviously, we are seeking deeper, second-order changes that affect not only surface conduct but also underlying cognitive structures, perhaps even biochemical functions. In the case of mood disorders, for instance, it has not been that clear whether anomalies in the neurological system produce depression, or whether it's the other way around—that depressed moods change the body's chemistry.

Psychoanalysts such as Appelbaum (1994) think of structural change as a relatively stable internal pattern by which an individual initiates behavioral and interpersonal growth. This is enduring change in her words, the kind that leads a previously shy, reclusive person to find friends, or a formerly depressed, self-destructive person to find life satisfaction. It results in alteration of the essential self.

There is some debate, at least among psychoanalysts, about exactly how structural changes may best be facilitated. While Kernberg (1984) and other traditional analysts believe that only profound interpretation can sufficiently penetrate defenses and unconscious processes to promote real change in the self, others such as Wallerstein (1986) believe that supportive therapeutic relationships may be sufficient to initiate underlying structural changes.

Once we leave the bounds of psychoanalytic thinking, there are hundreds of other theories to explain the best means for promoting structural changes. We will see later how these divergent approaches may actually be far more alike than they first appear.

Second-Order Change

Nowadays, we simply don't often have the time to think about deeper level, structural changes. The clock is running. Quality assurance teams and health maintenance organizations are watching our every move, second-guessing our treatment plans, and urging us to work faster and more efficiently. Administrators on restricted budgets want to see an uncomplicated, cause and effect relationship between a specific presenting problem and a subsequent therapeutic intervention that leads to immediate results. As mentioned earlier, these simple linear adjustments are considerably more modest than the deeper, structural changes in the core of a person's being (Lyddon, 1990). While the former aim for mere alleviation of targeted symptoms, the latter involves a radical, dramatic restructuring of a client's essential views of self and the world. Such sweeping, second-order changes occur mostly when a person's own equilibrium is threatened to a sufficient magnitude that major structural reorganization takes place (Hanna & Ritchie, 1995).

Most clinicians—if given a choice and the time—would much prefer to aim for deeper shifts in client functioning. Such work not only is more satisfying, but its effects are more likely to last longer when we have the opportunity to look at presenting problems in the larger context of a person's life. That is not to say that real, lasting changes only take place in so-called "deeper" therapies, just that learning tends to stick better when there are opportunities to practice new behaviors in controlled environments and to test new beliefs in supportive relationships.

State Versus Trait Conditions

It is also useful to think in terms of relatively temporary versus stable characteristics so that we may focus on targets that are most likely to respond to what therapists do. If we have one or two sessions to make a difference in a person's life, it would be far more efficient to work on current coping patterns rather than entrenched defense mechanisms. While "temporary" refers to the choices a person makes in dealing with his present predicament, "stable" involves characteristic tendencies that have been around for a very long time. Of course, changes in one of these domains can certainly lead to changes in the other.

Psychologists talk about "state" versus "trait" conditions in relation to learning and anxiety. With respect to trait change, that is, the kind that becomes a permanent part of the person, there are still state conditions that are conducive to a person's readiness and openness to transformation. These can include the following:

> *Distress.* When people are upset they feel anxious, depressed, or otherwise emotionally distraught. Such extreme moods inhibit personal functioning and interrupt daily routines.
>
> *Frustration tolerance.* This involves the ability of a person to deal with discomfort and learn from crisis situations.
>
> *Physiology.* This category includes anything related to the body's functioning—sleep, physical health, pregnancy, diet, drugs, or perceptual acuity.
>
> *Systemic transactions.* There is an interpersonal context to all problems encountered.
>
> *Cognitive conditions.* A person's internal belief system is often involved in the trouble, distorting or exaggerating what is happening.
>
> *Cultural context.* Gender, ethnicity, and other cultural factors also shape a person's perceptions and behavior.

Defensiveness. How guarded, controlled, or well-defended is the person?

Psychological environment. This refers to a person's susceptibility to influence from significant others, as well as contingencies and reinforcers.

Serendipity. Random or chance encounters also play a role in a person's readiness and openness to change.

Before attempting to initiate trait-level changes, it is often useful to work on state conditions first.

Three Other Kinds of Change

Of the classification systems for describing change, one typology is interesting because it was generated by clients in therapy. In one study (Cummings, Hallberg, & Selemon, 1994), clients in short-term therapy were asked to fill out questionnaires after each session about what made the most difference to them in the session. Participants described three kinds of change they experienced.

1. *Interrupted change* is a brief burst of progress followed by a return to previous patterns. This occurs when, for example, a client applies newly learned assertiveness skills at home, finds they produce negative results, and immediately abandons any further efforts along this path.
2. *Minimal change* is a modest gain that happens after initial resistance. At first, the client seems reluctant to experiment with alternative ways of responding to conflict. After learning a new way of handling a situation and practicing the method in session, he or she tries out the strategy with limited success.
3. *Consistent change* is stable, progressive, and permanent. The first two types can eventually lead to consistent change, but only if efforts are made to move beyond the surface structure.

This classification system makes it possible for us to communicate more precisely with clients (and colleagues) about the sort of goals we are working toward and the kind of progress that has been made.

Quantum Change

Consistent change is not unlike the second-order change described previously. To be even more precise, a particular kind of consistent change has been identified. Miller and C'deBaca (1994) coined the term "quantum" change to describe a sudden, unexpected, and dramatic shift that becomes permanent in a person's life. They refer initially to overnight spiritual transformations such as the cases of Dickins' Ebenezer Scrooge, Joan of Arc, Buddha, and Malcolm X. In each case, a life course was permanently altered as a result of a single crystallizing vision. As illustrated in the narratives of the previous chapter, this focal incident often involves an increased level of discontent (Baumeister, 1994).

To test the hypothesis that such changes are both possible and enduring, Miller and C'deBaca (1994) interviewed 55 people who reported such quantum changes. Over three fourths were caught completely by surprise and could still remember the exact date of the precipitating event. These occurrences, usually lasting less than a day, were precipitated by some external source. Even more impressive, when the subjects were asked how long the changes lasted, 80% reported that the effects were maintained completely over time, and the other 20% said that they "mostly lasted."

What sorts of events lead to such sudden, quantum shifts? Just as one might imagine, they involve potentially life-threatening situations, destabilizing events, or circumstances containing a spiritual element. Examples include a serious operation, a "moment of truth" during alcoholism rehabilitation, a religious conversion, and various kinds of trauma. The old adage, "that which does not kill you makes you stronger," seems to fit the narratives.

While Miller and C'deBaca don't claim to understand what conditions are most likely to promote such quantum changes, they strongly believe that acknowledging the possibility of such phenomena is an important first step. After all, they suggest, this type of change flies in the face of much conventional wisdom in our field that describes change as an evolutionary, developmental, and incremental process. Before therapists can hope to understand how and why quantum changes occur, we need an openness to recognize and acknowledge that this process is possible.

I think many, if not most people, have experienced a glimpse of quantum change at one time or another. Perhaps you have witnessed such a sudden personality shift in others, whether a family member or client. There may have been a recognizable moment of revelation, such as a look of enlightenment on a client's face. Even more convincing, however, are those times when *you* were forever changed as a result of a sudden, unexpected catalyst.

I remember the day, even the hour, when I learned to ride my two-wheel bicycle without training wheels. I remember looking down and seeing the cracks on the sidewalk, amazed that they were rolling by in a whirl of motion. I can still hear the sound of my father's voice, "Thatta way Jeffie. Thatta way!" And I remember the complete freedom that this mastered skill now represented in my life. I was no longer bound by my own block but could explore the whole neighborhood!

I remember the helplessness, the loss of control, and the suicidal desperation I felt when a college girlfriend ended our relationship. Walking out into a field, I thought about dying, then finally about living in a new way. By the time I walked back to my room, I was literally a new man.

I recall the evening I sat with six others in an igloo of our own creation. We were processing the day's activities, trying to survive on an Outward Bound adventure. I was challenged by one of our leaders for being so impatient and reluctant to wait for others to keep up, and realized that was a perfect metaphor for how trapped I felt in my life. At the time, I was in charge of a dozen other therapists and utterly sick of the responsibility. I knew at that moment that I would quit as soon as I returned home.

I can name numerous other quantum changes, but then I am a change junkie, so addicted to personal transformation that I can't stop writing about it. As a teacher and therapist, I also love experiencing it vicariously through the lives of my clients and students. What about you?

If a strong predictor of quantum change is the belief that it is indeed possible, then it is certainly a worthwhile endeavor to research this phenomenon for yourself. Review your own personal history for evidence that "overnight" change occurred as a result of some seminal event or moment of epiphany. Ask your clients about their own quantum changes, and just as important, how they believe those sudden shifts took place. Talk to friends and family members about their experiences along these lines. Finally, identify the most consistent variables present in these personal transformations.

Big and Little Changes

This book is concerned with quantum change. This means "big," rather than "little" change, and major transformations that produce constructive, enduring impact—not just in thinking, behavior, or attitudes, but in the whole person. Such higher levels of personal functioning become evident not just to oneself but also to others.

Mahoney (1991) speaks of the central paradox of change—the ways it aligns with a person's search for order and familiarity, as well as yearning for novelty. The deeper the change (measured by magnitude, intensity, and significance), the more it will be connected to a sense of personal meaning. Likewise, he cautions, "the more there will be natural, healthy, and vigorous resistance" (p. 34). Big changes often hurt—a lot.

No wonder we feel so ambivalent about change. On the one hand, we hunger for something new and different from what we already have. On the other hand, this condemns us to a state of disorientation and extreme discomfort. Beware of the client who talks incessantly about how much fun therapy is and how much he or she is learning. Some of the best work we do is ugly—very ugly. We seem to wield a sword rather than a scalpel, doing what it takes to excise poisonous tissue.

How Long Must It Take?

Two final factors to consider in our discussion are the magnitude of change (how much) and rate of change (how fast). These two variables are generally considered connected, with magnitude being greater according to certain rates of change. This can go in both directions. Fast change can produce the most powerful effects, such as in times of trauma or sudden critical incidents. Just as commonly, deeper level changes often take place slowly and incrementally.

Milton Erickson helped to spearhead the notion that big changes can occur very rapidly and not take a long time. Mahoney (1997) tells the story of his single session with the master trance specialist during a time in his life when he felt bewildered about a career choice. After 2 hours of listening to stories, Erickson inserted an enigmatic statement at the very end.

"Many times in the ensuing years," Mahoney relates, "I have reflected on those 2 hours and those last few minutes. His response to my dilemma was not a straightforward prescription or even a logical translation. But it was a powerful experience that influenced the trajectory of my life" (p. 28).

In spite of such dramatic shifts, Mahoney persists in the belief that lasting, significant change takes a fair amount of time. Indeed, even if our intervention is swift and incisive, it generally takes a while for the client to integrate matters and personalize them in such a way that they become internalized.

It is not that second-order, quantum, big changes must necessarily take years of treatment; they can be launched in one conversation, sometimes in a single remark or incident. But what makes the effects last? That is the real question we are addressing. Before we investigate the factors that contribute most to enduring changes, we will explore the variables that most often sabotage such efforts.

4
CHAPTER

Why Changes Don't Last

It is New Year's Day—a time for resolutions. At this time of year I take inventory of who I am, where I've been, and where I'm going. For the 14th year in a row, I come face-to-face with aspects of myself I want to change.

After years in therapy, as both a client and a clinician, I realize only too well the recurrent themes that play themselves out in my life, inhibiting greater pleasure and interfering with a sense of inner peace. I am impatient and driven, always striving for recognition and achievement in the hope that I will finally prove myself good enough for ... approval, self-acceptance, whatever.

Every year, as the calendar starts over, I resolve to do some things differently. I want to slow down, relax more, and spend less money. I use all the methods that I teach others in order to make these changes happen, and they do occur for a little while. They just don't stick. What does it take to make resolutions, formed with the most sincere commitment, last?

Why People Change

It is helpful to start by examining why people want to change in the first place. Four possibilities immediately come to mind.

1. *Something is broken.* Often, people don't want to change—they have to. Most don't begin therapy just because they want a little refinement

49

in their life. They are usually desperate, having exhausted all other alternatives. They believe that something is terribly wrong, something that they cannot fix on their own.

2. *Boredom.* People become tired of things the way they are and hunger for something different. They long for stimulation, diversity, or a break in their routines. They are willing to stir things up just to enjoy a little action, even if it means they will put themselves in an uncomfortable position.

3. *Growth and development.* Inevitable transitions and turning points in life force us to make new accommodations and adjustments. The aging process, for example, requires people to learn other ways to get their needs met. A creaking back, poor eyesight, or reduced bladder functions certainly gets one's attention.

4. *Critical incidents.* People don't always go looking for change; sometimes it finds them. In the case of traumas and critical incidents, for example, perhaps there is a precondition that makes a person ripe for transformation, but the actual process may be sparked by some external event.

There were other themes evident in the earlier stories of transformation, but these four categories cover most of the territory. Change is generally the result of a complex series of events and circumstances that are only partially related to a person's choices and decisions.

The Limits of Intention

The world is filled with individuals making honorable resolutions. According to George Bernard Shaw, the road to hell is also paved with good intentions. Many people mean well. They intend to do things that are good for themselves or others, but somewhere along the line they become distracted or led astray.

The sayings of poets and philosophers regarding change are also supported by research. In a review of empirical studies on the role of good intentions in promoting lasting change, Gollwitzer (1999) concludes that without some sort of constructive plan of action, as well as structured opportunities to attain desired objectives, commitment alone leads to frustration.

Not all intentional behavior, however, is equally futile. Much depends on how promises are made, as well as how goals are defined and constructed. For instance, efforts are more likely to fail when *declared goals* relate to ultimate performance rather than learning specific behavior or task (Dweck, 1996). A client is less likely to meet the goal of asking someone out for a date during the coming week than the intention of practicing assertiveness skills learned during the session.

Enduring results are also not likely if stated intentions are too general and vague, such as, "I will try to do my best" (Gollwitzer, 1999; Locke & Latham, 1990). Even more relevant to our subject is the finding that while the reaching of promotion goals is dependent on the presence or absence of some positive outcome, preventing relapses depends on negative outcomes (Higgins, 1997). Thus, maintaining changes is much harder than making initial changes.

Time and time again we have seen people declare, with utmost enthusiasm and seriousness, that they intend to do various things differently in the future. Such intentions, while certainly fully committed at the time, are not nearly enough to sustain future momentum. There are a number of very good reasons why people say they want to be different but are unable to follow through with their declarations.

☐ Why People Resist Change

One of the most frustrating parts of our jobs is working with people who don't really want what we are selling. They may be referred for treatment against their will or blackmailed into coming under threat of dire consequences. They may say they are delighted and eager to participate in the process (they might even believe this themselves) but will do everything in their power to make sure that things stay basically the same. There are a number of good reasons why people tend to resist change. The following factors often play a prominent role (Bunker & De Lisle, 1991; Kottler, 1992):

- *Lack of awareness that change is needed.* People can remain blissfully and spectacularly ignorant about their most self-defeating behaviors. They can remain in denial, even in the face of overwhelming evidence that their efforts are counter-productive. In such cases, people either don't know how they are perceived because they don't pay very good attention or they don't listen to what people are telling them. In either case, they don't change because they don't realize that such adjustments are necessary. "Sure," a client may reluctantly admit, "people tell me all the time that what I'm doing is not working, but I just figured that they were the ones with the problem."
- *Inability to decide what needs to be done.* A person may readily acknowledge that something needs to change but he or she can't decide which course of action to take. The individual remains frozen, torn between choices, unable or unwilling to risk being wrong. In the case of multi-

ple persons involved in a struggle, change can be averted indefinitely as long as a consensus cannot be reached.

- *Lack of understanding of what is expected.* This person truly wants to change but does not know what is required in the situation. This is not indicative of resistance to change, but rather to lack of awareness about factors involved. Sometimes therapists feel frustrated because clients are not cooperating when, in fact, the clients are doing the best they can. Clients come to us with unrealistic and inaccurate beliefs about what we can and cannot do on their behalf. It is our job to correct these misconceptions in such a way that they don't run away out of disappointment.

- *Inability to do what is expected.* A client may very well want to change and may even understand all too well what must be done. The main problem, however, is that he or she does not have the skills, ability, or wherewithal to complete the task. While the problem in the previous factor lies in the faulty assumptions of the client, here the trouble is lodged in the therapist's erroneous beliefs. We may assume that a client can access certain feelings, reflect on some interpretation, or follow through on steps toward a declared goal. In reality, the person may lack the preparation, training, or knowledge to respond as we would prefer.

- *Lack of willingness to give up what is perceived as valuable.* Every change involves not only gaining something, but also losing something. In many cases, what is lost may not be all that useful or effective, but it is familiar and comfortable. Changing a grip on a tennis racket or golf club, for instance, means initially feeling awkward when the new grip is compared to the previous one. The ball may not have been traveling very straight, or very hard, but at least the swing felt comfortable.

- *Reinforcement for remaining the same.* People tend to repeat dysfunctional patterns and resist changing them because they receive some benefit for remaining the same. The drunk can hide. The whiner can blame others. The guilt-ridden can get sympathy and attention. The secondary gains of the self-defeating behavior are so attractive that it seems senseless to sacrifice those pay-offs for some, as yet, undetermined benefits. The symptomatic behavior may have certain undesirable side effects, but it also provides a fair degree of power and control.

- *Lack of belief that what is offered is better than the status quo.* The person remains unconvinced that change presents significant advantages over what he or she is already doing. When all is said and done, it doesn't appear as if the alternative plan is any better than the present method of operating. A client may be stuck in what seems to us a very dysfunctional and abusive relationship, but when contemplating single life, it does not seem so bad to the client after all.

- *Feeling threatened by the anticipated outcome.* Whether it is outside of our conscious awareness or not, change is usually accompanied by a degree of threat. There are risks involved. There are unknown and perhaps dangerous consequences lurking around the corner. Maybe current circumstances aren't so bad after all.
- *A low personal tolerance for change.* Everyone has a different predisposition for adaptability. Some people embrace change while others avoid it all costs because of prior negative experiences or poor adaptive skills.
- *Tendency to cooperate in a way that is different from what others prefer or expect.* This is one of my favorites, one I like to remind myself of often. I sometimes question whether concepts such as "resistance" are valid or are merely labels attached to behavior by those in power (such as therapists) when they are not happy with the way things are proceeding. Time after time when a therapist complains to me about an obstructive, resistant client, I see just as often that it is the therapist who is being difficult because of his or her unwillingness to adapt to the client's needs and personal style.

I believe that all clients do the best they can to cooperate with us, given where they are at the time, and what they are ready and able to do. The hard part for us is to abandon our own comfortable preferences and agendas in lieu of strategies that may be more flexible and that honor the particular client's needs at that moment in time. I don't mean to imply that some awfully obnoxious, toxic folks don't end up in our offices, many of whom absolutely love playing games. But even these so-called difficult clients are doing the best they can to cope with situations that are very threatening and frightening.

☐ The Benefits of Regression

Relapses, regressions, and other returns to previous functioning occur most often when the individual is not able—or not willing—to maintain progress. I have been speaking as if lasting change is the only satisfactory outcome when, in fact, there are sometimes good reasons why changes are not continued.

- *The person is not prepared to maintain the changes.* More skills, training, or experience may be required. More preparation and practice may be indicated. The client may be sending clear signals that he or she is not yet ready to move to the next stage. Some forms of treatment, such as psychoanalysis, are designed, in fact, to promote regression out of a belief that one must return to previously unresolved issues before proceeding forward with sustained changes (Kirschner & Kirschner, 1991).

- *The changes attempted are not realistic or practical.* This is related to the earlier point that people may be asked to take action with which they are not able or willing to comply. The changes don't last because the person is just not capable of maintaining them, given the circumstances.
- *The outcome is not what the person really wants after all.* Sometimes people discover that they really don't want what they thought they wanted.
- *The outcome may have been desired, but it is not what is really needed.* It may require too much effort and energy to maintain the changes. In a cost-benefit analysis, the outcome is not worth the expenditure.
- *The change is good for the individual but not for others in his or her life.* Things may be improved for the person initiating the change, but others may be suffering as a result.

All of these points act as a reminder that sometimes changes don't last because they are really not what the person needs or wants. Such a possibility must be not only considered but also respected.

☐ How Lasting Change is Sabotaged

Now that we have examined the reasons why some people resist change, we can now look more carefully at what contributes most to sabotaging progress after it has begun. These factors include those within the individual and those within the social context of the person's world.

Lousy Goals

Most change efforts are doomed to fail because the goals selected are unrealistic, or even impossible, to maintain in the first place. A client may say that she intends to avoid all chronic overspending and impulsive purchases in the future, but she has taken few incremental steps toward this objective and has virtually no previous success in accomplishing it. Moreover, this behavior may be serving numerous functions in her life, including that of "self-medication" for loneliness and anxiety. Although she may be able to cease her spending behavior for a period of days, or even a few weeks, the chances of maintaining the "cure" for the rest of her life are negligible.

As in the case of so many good intentions, the probability that change efforts will succeed are often related to the ways the target behaviors are defined and selected. We greatly increase the likelihood that clients can reach their desired objectives but structuring them in reasonable, incremental, and attainable steps.

Dysfunctional Beliefs

The probability of attaining and maintaining goals is related to both the quality of the original resolution (having clear reasons) and the degree of commitment (remembering the reasons). When someone has a defeatist attitude ("This probably won't last long."), progress is also unlikely over the long haul.

In their manual on relapse prevention in the treatment of addictive disorders, Wanigaratne and several colleagues (1990) list some of the most common faulty beliefs that prevent lasting change:

Overgeneralization. "Because I had one drink, this means *I am* a drunk." This is also called the "rule violation effect" (Marlatt & Gordon, 1985), which proves to be a self-fulfilling prophecy. If someone believes, "once a drunk, always a drunk," then this prediction is more likely to be true.

Discounting. This occurs when people attend selectively to negative aspects of the situation: "Sure I managed to do the homework on time, but I did a lousy job."

Mind-reading. People get themselves in trouble when they make erroneous assumptions about others: "My boss was probably thinking it was too late anyway."

Fortune telling. This is another type of inaccurate, self-defeating prediction, emphasizing negative outcomes: "If I tell him what we talked about, he will still just ignore me."

Magnification. This involves blowing things out of proportion: "I have never had such an awful experience in my whole life. I can't believe I was embarrassed in front of everyone."

Disasterization. This occurs when people allow themselves to imagine the worst possible outcome: "Well, I can try doing things the way we've talked about, but I know that it will only make the situation worse."

Emotional reasoning. People sometimes think things through in a distorted, illogical way as a result of feeling clouded and overwhelmed: "Because I feel ashamed, I must give up and not try again."

Self-labeling. People may think about and describe themselves in absolute terms based on a few samples of behavior: "I'm a shy person."

Personalization. This involves taking too much responsibility for results: "It was all my fault. If only I hadn't said what I did, things would never have reached this point."

Musterbation. This involves the use of "musts" or "shoulds" and demanding that the world be a certain way: "I must succeed with this every time or there is no sense in even trying."

Perfectionism. People have very unrealistic expectations for themselves and others: "Sure I did a pretty good job, but it's not like me to screw up like that."

In addition to these common cognitive traps, Prochaska, Norcross, & DiClemente (1994) found in their study of people who make lasting changes that those who are overconfident and prone to self-blame get in trouble the most. Thus, whether or not we are cognitively-oriented therapists, sensitizing ourselves to the previously mentioned "thought disturbances" that foreshadow later problems would be useful. It is even more helpful to encourage clients to monitor their own self-sabotaging thinking patterns, either through internal dialogue or systematic entries in a journal.

Developmental Readiness

Another reason that change doesn't persist is the lack of an internal infrastructure to support it. For instance, parents are known to force their children to do tricks to accelerate their motor skills development that don't actually affect their future mastery of these skills. If we try to promote changes in adults before they are developmentally ready, there will be inevitable slips backward. This may be related to the cognitive, personality, emotional, physical, moral, or even career stage in which a person may be presently operating.

A client who desperately wants to be involved in an intimate, loving relationship with a potential new suitor asks you to see them together to help shepherd the relationship toward this goal. Before you agree to this agenda you do a little background check and find that this woman has never been involved in a long-term relationship, is still very sexually and romantically naive, and has even been sexually abused by her older brother as a child. Even if you could be successful in helping them negotiate a high degree of intimacy, the long-term prognosis, given the circumstances, would not be great without sufficient preparation. Although this client may say she is ready for such a relationship, and may very well mean it, she needs time to catch up emotionally and perhaps physically.

Cultural Upbringing

During a recent 6-month visit to Iceland, I got to talking with a woman who is a counselor, or at least training to be one. Gudrun Kristinsdottir seemed quiet when I first met her, as many Icelanders tend toward reserve and shyness when they encounter foreigners in their land. In talking about the experiences that most shaped the person she is today, she immediately thought of her upbringing as an example of how change is resisted.

"It was because I was brought up on a small, isolated island called Vestmannaeyjar, off the Southern coast of Iceland, that I am the way I am. I didn't realize this for certain until I left my home and moved elsewhere. I was sent to boarding school in Akureyri, far away from where I grew up. Soon I discovered that I did not speak the same language as the other children and the way I expressed myself led to misunderstandings."

Gudrun (pronounced a bit like *Gvith-run*) smiles as she thinks about her first experiences on the main island. "In Vestmannaeyjar I was used to saying what I thought about things and to speaking clearly to avoid misunderstandings. Most jobs in my village were connected to fishing in some way and almost all the men in my family were sailors. I was very much influenced by this, so I tended to swear a lot and use rude words."

It was being thrust in an alien culture that forced Gudrun to face her differentness from others. The ways she ordinarily expressed herself now got her in trouble. She felt like she had lost something of herself because she had to be so careful about what she said, and how she said it.

"In Akureyri, my new home, a man named Jon (pronounced *Yone*) was just called Jon." That did not tell me anything about him though. In Vestmannaeyjar we used to add some meaning to people's names and everyone had something added that said something more about who they were."

I was very confused by this custom, not at all sure what she was talking about. When I cocked my head in puzzlement, Gudrun elaborated further.

"Yes, I know. People think this sounds strange and outsiders actually consider us rude and mean. But this is not at all the way it is meant. It's just natural that people's names should say something more about them then just what they are called."

Again, I looked puzzled so Gudrun supplied some examples.

"I remember a man named Jon med fjallid, or Jon the Mountain. That was because he had such a huge nose. And when Edmund Hillary climbed Mount Everest, his name became Jon Everest. Gudjon Flaekingur,

Gudjon the vagabond, got his name when he was offered a job on the mainland and he moved there with his family. In a short while he came back and was never called anything but Gudjon the vagabond after that. An unusually tall man was called Gvendur Afturmastur—Gvendur the mast. Steini Gurka was Steini the cucumber because he had moved to our town from Hveragerdi where he had grown vegetables. My next-door neighbor was called Ingimundur 111 because he took snuff and could not keep it in his nose, so it constantly ran into his mouth in three streamlets. So you see that names in my mind should be more than just names."

I nodded my understanding in between giggles at this lovely custom.

"I still use this method with people, although I've learned to do it just in my mind."

Gudrun feels the powerful imprint of her home culture as the strongest force that molded her personality and resists change, even when living in a different place. This is, of course, true of all of us. We have all been "imprinted" by our various cultural influences, including our home life, ethnicity, religion, socioeconomic background, gender, and so on. Although at times we might want to reshape or reinvent ourselves, doing so often feels like we are constantly swimming upstream against a very strong current.

Personality Traits

People are born with certain traits that predispose them to varying degrees of flexibility and hardiness (Florian, Mikulincer, & Taubman, 1995). The same is true for levels of frustration tolerance and resilience. In addition, the dimensions of a *Diagnostic and Statistical Manual of Mental Disorders* (DSM) "Axis II" personality disorder make some people so self-centered, manipulative, distracted, encapsulated, or entrenched in other stable patterns that it requires a herd of wild therapists—I mean horses—to pull them out of the mire in which they are stuck.

When therapists base a treatment summary on a DSM Axis II diagnosis, they often find that most insurance companies are very reluctant to pay for services. The general consensus seems to be that such personality disorders are so intractable and impervious to change that treatment is not seen as worthwhile, or at least cost-effective. While such clients are hardly the hopeless cause that insurance administrators might lead us to believe, we would have to agree that some people do require considerable time in order for significant changes to be observed. Even so, there is a far greater likelihood that the changes won't stick for long.

Negative Moods

Collins (1999) describes the long-standing struggle of a 22-year-old woman with eating disorders since high school to overcome her nemesis. In attempts to stabilize herself, she has seen 11 different therapists. She has worked on body image, self esteem, and feelings of perfectionism. She has taken antidepressant medications. She has read hundreds of books and tried every known remedy, only to find that initial progress has never lasted very long. "My disease festers and spreads like a cancer," she says, "and spreads through my soul. I get sick of fighting it every day, every minute ... the more I try to keep it hidden, the stronger it seems to grow."

It wasn't until she became pregnant that she finally found incentives to stay on track. But I would be hesitant to say that she is cured. "I would like to think that someday I could be totally healed, but I think it's more like alcoholism. You are never a recovered anorexic or bulimic ... only a recovering one."

Is this disorder really a disease, or is it the belief that this is so that makes it reality for her? Many other ex-bingers and purgers now lead normal eating lives, without much thought of their self-destructive pasts. Perhaps it is the presence of a mood disorder that makes it so much more difficult for some people to recover permanently. When this woman feels a depressive spell come upon her, the behaviors connected with her disorder make her feel better, temporarily. In spite of her intentions, she acts impulsively, her behavior elicited by mood states apparently out of her control. In addition, she struggles with a distorted body image, perceptual and cognitive distortions, and secondary benefits she enjoys as a result of her "disease."

It is no wonder that her prognosis is so poor. Others who are emotionally distraught or crippled by severe depression or acute anxiety also experience new changes as being particularly susceptible to relapse. They lack motivation, confidence, and a sense of focus. All of their efforts are expended getting out of bed in the morning and keeping active throughout the day which leaves little time or energy for worrying about "luxury" items like continuing change efforts.

Attribution of Blame

If a problem is not one's fault, if it results from circumstances outside one's control (e.g., bad weather, poor genes, vindictive boss, bad luck, fate, lousy breaks, conspiracy of the universe), then much less personal responsibility can be exerted to control the outcome.

Unless clients are willing to assume some responsibility for their behavior, as well as for the outcomes, it is very difficult for them to make needed adjustments to improve performance. The great thing about blaming external factors is that it protects clients from really having to do anything differently. That is also, of course, the unfortunate aspect of such a cognitive strategy.

Much of the work we do in therapy certainly involves helping people examine how their own beliefs and personal narratives have been influenced by societal forces, often against their will (Monk, Winslade, Crocket, & Epston, 1997; Neimeyer, 1995). Yet another important task is to help people realize how they can become authors of their own experience, not only in rewriting their pasts but in crafting their futures. This process can hardly be successful if we can't convince them to examine the impact of the choices they make and the behavior in which they engage.

It is one thing to blame, quite legitimately, the forces of oppression that have limited choices and options available because of one's gender, minority status, or cultural upbringing. It is another to use this as an excuse for rarely taking charge of one's own life. Our difficult task as therapists is to help people to recognize and acknowledge the influences that have held them back, but also to move forward by cutting those strings.

Perceptual Deficits

One important reason why people fail to maintain changes is because they don't recognize the first signs of deterioration—the early warning system alerting them that they are in danger of relapsing. This can take place because they are not suitably prepared to recognize such cues, but can also be the result of certain deficits.

Fatigue for instance, can be a factor. When people are tired, they are less likely to pick up on risky temptations. Other physiological deficits, such as the lack of requisite visual or auditory acuity to pick up on cues that signal impending problems, can also make maintenance more difficult.

I remember one client who was constantly getting into trouble because she was late for appointments. She lost jobs after arriving late for important meetings. True to form, she was late for each of our sessions, arriving predictably 20 minutes after our scheduled appointment time. She was always apologetic about these lapses and seemed at a loss to explain them.

At first, I took things personally and interpreted her behavior as resistance to treatment, then later as a form of acting out and unexpressed aggression. Soon it became apparent that this late behavior had been a problem her whole life, even when she genuinely wanted to arrive at a particular place on time.

Just for the heck of it, during one session I decided to test her ability to make time estimates. I sent her to the drinking fountain down the hall after asking her to predict how long this task would take. She guessed about a minute (it took four). As she was leaving that day, I asked her how long it would take to get to her car in the parking lot after she left my office. She estimated three minutes (it took six). As a little assignment, I asked her to continue writing down time estimates for every task she completed during the day. She discovered that almost every prediction was about half the time the task actually took. Her "cure" to the problem involved simply doubling her estimate of how long it would take to do something. Lo and behold, for the first time in a dozen sessions, she showed up to the next appointment two minutes early. I remain convinced that this woman had a perceptual deficit related to time estimation that impaired her ability to conduct the daily affairs of her life efficiently.

Lack of Coping Skills

Unless we prepare our clients for inevitable setbacks and lapses, acknowledge that they occur, and equip them with what they need to recognize and respond to trouble, progress will often grind to a halt. This is something for which we are often unprepared ourselves. Almost all of our training was devoted to how to promote changes rather than how to make them last. Every treatment effort should thus prepare clients for the times when they will struggle.

Deke had been struggling for quite some time with an addiction to pornographic videos that dominated his life. He masturbated several times each day, always to his growing collection of movies. It had gotten to the point at which he was no longer interested in socializing, much less going out with women. His isolation became even more pronounced.

Deke responded rather quickly to intervention. He was highly motivated to give up his habit and agreed within a matter of weeks to destroy his collection. He thought it would even be helpful to stop masturbating altogether as a way of building sufficient tension to encourage him to initiate more contacts with women.

Deke was feeling so optimistic that he decided to end therapy and continue efforts on his own. This termination occurred, however, before there was any chance to work through how he would handle temptations to revert back to old patterns that were so easy for him. Sure enough, the first time he felt rejected after approaching a woman (she didn't respond as enthusiastically as he had hoped, more than actually reject him), he walked out of the bar and stopped at a video store on the way home. When he returned to treatment, it was with considerably less optimism that he would ever be able to control his impulses.

Secondary Gains of Dysfunctional Behavior

As mentioned earlier, people stay stuck or regress back to old ways because they enjoy the benefits of doing so. Becoming healthy comes with a certain amount of responsibility and hard work. It is often easier to revert to dysfunctional patterns that provide a way out of such requirements.

Giving up on change efforts and returning to previous maladaptive behavior often have the following benefits (Kottler, 1992):

1. Continued procrastination and avoidance of the unknown.
2. Maintenance of the status quo and avoidance of risks.
3. Permission to avoid responsibility. Notice how good it feels to say, "It's not my fault" and "I can't help it."
4. A sense of power. Destruction happens on your own terms and attention and sympathy are also readily available.

Bringing these secondary gains to the client's attention often helps to neutralize their effects. After all, it's much harder to get away with deceiving yourself after your methods have been brought into conscious awareness.

Lack of a Support System

It is not easy to continue engaging in self-defeating behavior in the face of reality that tells you that behavior is not working very well, or at least has some undesirable side effects. Wachtel (1991) contends that remaining dysfunctional is "hard, dirty work that cannot by successfully achieved alone" (p. 21).

Such problematic behavior is maintained through "accomplices" who are "recruited" or "trained" to protect people from the anguish of change. For instance, the most common cause of relapse among recovering teenage addicts is being around friends who are still using substances (Jaffee, 1992). There is, thus, a collaborative effort involved to sabotage progress over time. In the field of addictions, friends and relatives who unconsciously (or deliberately) conspire to encourage relapses so they don't have to change either are referred to as "enablers." A spouse, for example, may say with conviction that he desperately wants his wife to stop drinking, but then he buys her favorite wine to keep around the house. "What's wrong with that?" he says innocently. "Why should I stop enjoying wine?"

Change persists when it is reinforced and supported in the person's world. One reason that therapy has never worked very well with certain problems, including addictions and impulse disorders, is that the sessions represent only 1% of a client's waking hours. As soon as the client walks out the door, another set of influences come into play, many of which sabotage the best of intentions.

One of the best predictors of lasting personal change is the extent of social and family support available in the form of information, caring, positive attention, and greater intimacy (Zenmore & Shepel, 1989; Keniasty & Norris, 1995; Schaefer & Moos, 1998). When such resources are not readily accessible, it is the therapist's job to help create ongoing support networks once the therapy sessions end.

Self-Regulating Capacity

Family therapists and systems theorists were not the first to draw parallels between the physical world and human behavior, but they certainly popularized the idea that forces like equilibrium exert a powerful influence on organizational stability. In order to maintain homeostasis, efforts to protect the self from change take place actively and naturally at the most cellular level.

Recent evidence has shown that most people perceive themselves as having much more control over their lives and free will to manage their behavior than they really do (Park, 1999). As much as we would prefer to believe that initiating and maintaining change is merely about possessing sufficient willpower, in fact, everyday behavior is more often regulated by unconscious desires, choices made beyond awareness, and hidden environmental controls. We are programmed to respond automatically, without conscious thought, in order to save time and energy (Bargh & Chartrand, 1999). These "mental butlers," designed to organize our lives, become habituated to the point that they actually groove neurological pathways, which makes the prospect of long-term change quite bleak. After all, how do you change behavior over which you do not have conscious control?

The Limits of Will

According to our mythology, poetry, and historical legacy, human beings are capable of great acts of personal determination. We are in charge of our own destiny, possessors of great willpower, and masters of our own future. If we don't like the way things are going in our lives—no problem—we can simply make the needed changes.

There may be talk of fate, instincts, and genetics, but we most often prefer to conceive of ourselves as beings who are exempt from the laws of the universe. We can tame nature, harness gravity, build cozy dwellings with technological devices that protect us from any discomfort.

Therapists, in particular, often espouse the most optimistic platitudes imaginable, echoing the Nike slogan: "Just Do It!" We tell people things like:

- "Anything is possible."
- "It is up to you."
- "You are the one in charge of your own life."
- "You have to just try harder."
- "You are the only thing getting in the way of your dreams."
- "In order to make it happen, first you have to imagine it the way you want it to be."

Therapy is often based on the assumption that people can make whatever changes they need to make in order to improve the quality of their lives. Whatever has to be done—learn a new skill, change a bad habit, confront an adversary, alter perceptions or attitudes—a little training and practice will fix that right up.

As we have seen, reality is far more daunting. Many powerful forces work to prevent lasting change, just as gravity humbles the most enthusiastic flyer. Once change lasts for a while, it is no longer change but rather the status quo. At that point, people start to take things for granted and may become lazy and inattentive. Before they know it, they have taken a fall, without having seen the trap or temptation until it was too late.

In spite of all these factors and forces that make lasting change a difficult proposition, we can take steps to maximize the potential for an enduring effect. It all begins with an understanding of the process by which any change takes place.

5

Some Universal Features of Change Efforts

This chapter examines some of the most universal features of effective change efforts, including those that take place in a classroom, therapy session, work setting, or solo adventure. It builds upon the conceptual research begun by the author over 10 years ago (Kottler, 1986; 1991). Essentially, all change efforts involve similar variables that have been identified (Asay & Lambert, 1999; Curtis & Stricker, 1991; Hubble, Duncan, & Miller, 1999; Kottler, 1991; Norcross & Goldfried, 1992; Prochaska, Norcross, and DiClemente, 1994).

In an exploratory study of what produces second-order, structural changes in a client's core being, Hanna and Ritchie (1995) found, not surprisingly, incredible complexity in the phenomena involved. The most significant active ingredients—a supportive relationship, changes in thinking, a sense of necessity, developing a new perspective, confronting the problem, deciding to change—are familiar components of most therapeutic systems.

It's About Time For Good News

So far, much of the discussion has been about how dismal the prospects are for maintaining changes over time, given all the obstacles, distractions, and challenges along the way. In fact, most gains made in therapy do endure. In a review of hundreds of studies conducted to date,

65

Asay and Lambert (1999) conclude optimistically that not only do the vast majority of people (well over 75%) make relatively rapid progress (most in under 6 months and half within 10 sessions), but these efforts tend to persist. This data seem to conflict with previous research, mainly because most of the relapse studies were done with the most difficult sorts of problems—addictions and impulse disorders. For other complaints, however, changes can indeed be maintained under certain conditions.

It is, of course, often difficult to measure the effects of interventions since clients may delude themselves or be less than perfectly honest. Those people who report to us that they have made and continued the most significant progress are sometimes lying, just as others who report that they are failing miserably may be doing far better than they imagine.

I have lost count of the number of times a client reported to me that he was not making any progress at all, only to hear that family members are absolutely stunned by the differences they observe. Just as frequent are those instances when clients perform magnificently in session but really do not do much at all once they walk out the door. "Oh, I can't thank you enough," a client may say as she departs. "This therapy is the best thing that ever happened to me and I can't tell you how grateful I am for all the help you have given me." Before we pat ourselves on the back, we must cautiously recall that what this person is saying might not jive at all with what is going on in the outside world.

Putting aside doubts regarding the accuracy of client self-reports, most experienced therapists are not surprised by empirical studies that report that therapy works quite well in the vast majority of cases, and that the effects do appear to last. There are, naturally, consistent exceptions. Clients most vulnerable to relapse—substance abusers, and those with eating disorders, personality disorders, and chronic depression—are people whose problems are related to controlling impulses or coping with inherent dispositions. These groups also form a significant percentage of the people we are charged to help.

Planning For Long-Term Change

In order to maximize the likelihood of maintained progress in therapy, or any self-help change effort, it is critical to plan for this outcome as part of the intervention. Two variables were found to discriminate most reliably between people who keep their New Year's resolutions and those who don't (Norcross, Ratzin, & Payne, 1989). First, behavior persisted most often when people made preparations for their proposed changes ahead of time. They told friends and family what they were planning to do. They took definite steps to plan for what was about to take place, such as discarding all alcohol or tobacco in the house or purchasing clothes in a more optimistic size. Second, those whose changes were maintained showed higher levels of confidence in their decision to change, manifesting greater self-efficacy and less self-doubt.

Although this study's sample size was small and its methodology less than perfect, the results support what clinicians have often observed— that the more long-term planning that is undertaken for change, the more likely that it will last. Just as important is to attack lingering doubts and boost confidence so that clients can believe strongly in their own powers of resilience and endurance.

Asay and Lambert (1999) found that the optimal strategy for promoting ongoing change was one in which the final sessions of treatment focused on preventing and preparing for relapses. I would advocate for planning such outcomes from the very beginning of the therapeutic relationship by talking continuously about not only how things need to change but how efforts will be made to keep the progress going.

Imagine that you are seeing a new client who complains of loneliness and depression that she ascribes to a series of unsuccessful relationships. When you collect some basic history, you find that she has indeed been in one destructive relationship after another, beginning the next one before the previous one ends. She has never really been alone in her life for any extended period of time. She married the first time to escape her crazy home life, and then had an affair to escape the marriage that was even worse than what she had at home. Although the affair didn't last long, it provided a bridge until her next partner came along, a chronic gambler and drinker. When this relationship petered out, she desperately attached herself to the next guy who came along who wasn't too bad at all: "He was just a little strange. We never had sex much because he preferred other means of satisfaction. But at least he never hit me." That live-in relationship had just come to an end and now she was living alone for the first time as an adult.

When asked what she wants out of the therapy, you are surprised by how perceptive, honest, and insightful the woman is about her ongoing pattern. She tells you quite directly that she already realizes that she has been reluctant to face life on her own rather than depending on a crummy relationship. She also is quite frank about the ongoing power of this revelation: "Look, I know I've got to learn to take care of myself. I also know that I've made some bad choices in the past about who I got involved with. I don't trust my judgement in these matters. But I also know that in spite of my intentions to work on this problem with you, if another man comes along in the meantime, I might just connect up with him. You gotta admit—it's a lot easier."

You admit that, in the short run, this is indeed the case. While you gather your thoughts and decide what to say to this client and how you will plan your treatment with her, you decide to bring up the challenge of enduring change from this first session.

"By your own admission," you tell her, "your prognosis isn't so great. You don't have a lot of faith in your ability to sustain your motivation. You can't really picture yourself at a time in the future when you will be able to function on your own, and when you can make better choices regarding your love relationships. And that is particularly worrisome to me because the best predictor of lasting change is something called "self-efficacy," which means essentially that you expect to change and that you have reasonable confidence in your ability to reach your goals and maintain them over time."

Well, this certainly gets her attention. She looks even more glum than before she came in.

"So," she says in a very quiet voice, "you're saying that there is no hope for me? You're saying that you can't help me?"

"Oh no," you quickly reassure her, "quite the contrary. I think that we could make a lot of progress together. But I just want you to think about, from the very beginning, that our efforts are not aimed at simply getting rid of your annoying symptoms of loneliness and depression right now. I know they are disturbing to you and you don't like feeling this way, so much so that you feel those same old impulses to hook up with the next man you meet. The first place we must begin our work is to plan not only to help you feel better again, but also to prevent such a circumstance in the future."

One of the most powerful things we can tell a client is that whatever we do in session doesn't matter nearly as much as what he or she does outside the therapy. Change is meaningful when conversations are applied to real-life situations, and when this learning is generalized to other aspects of personal functioning. Furthermore, "real" change occurs only when the effects persist.

☐ The Universal Features of Lasting Change

Now we arrive at the core of our subject—the essence of what makes changes last. Two conditions are usually present during all successful change efforts (Lambert & Bergin, 1994):

- Intentional efforts are made to plan for the long haul rather than just resolve acute problems.
- Individuals attribute the changes they made to their own power and effort rather than to external causes.

These variables, however, are just a few of those most often associated with relatively permanent changes. Prochaska (1999) has also plotted the process into several distinct stages:

1. *Thinking about it.*

   Anyone who has initiated a divorce or ended a long-standing relationship knows that such a decision often takes years to germinate before leading to definitive action. At first, there is denial. Then other defenses kick in, such as rationalizing that things aren't nearly as bad as they seem. At the point of taking the most drastic step, most people have exhausted all other options. They build up resolve and courage, ruminate and second-guess themselves, and often procrastinate. Mostly, they think about things over and over to make certain of what they want.

2. *Intending to do something about it.*

   Before action comes intention. After a decision is made to do something, a plan outlining what will be done and how it will be done is necessary. This is still a reflective period, but one in which the person has pretty much decided to change. This is a time for planning, yet it is often accompanied by a certain degree of hesitance, or procrastination.

   In some cases, relative ignorance can lead one to underestimate the challenges that lie ahead. I was teaching a course in career development that required students to present the major theories in the field. One team of students produced a video demonstrating Anne Roe's theory of the impact of early childhood dreams on later development. They interviewed people on the street, as well as a group of five-year-olds.

   One adorable little girl with huge eyes and poise beyond her years answered simply that when she grew up the job she wanted most was to be a princess. To their credit, the interviewers didn't crack a smile, but followed up with the question, "So, how does one become a princess?"

   "It's easy," the little girl replied. "You just get a pretty dress and a crown."

   In one sense, that does seem like the type of major miscalculation a five-year-old would make about attaining the position of a princess. Yet on the other hand, the more I think about her simple statement, the more true it seems. The goal of wanting to *be* something starts first with the intention, which reduces the objective to its simplest form.

3. *Taking action.*

   This is the point at which a person finally does change. There is a leap of faith, with all the usual misgivings. In addition to excitement, there is also apprehension, doubt, and fear. The change is fresh and unstable. Without adequate support and reinforcement, the effects won't last very long and regression is highly likely.

4. *Maintaining progress.*

The final stage, essentially the subject of this book, involves the important element of maintenance of change over time. This period usually lasts from 6 months to 5 years after the initial changes are implemented.

The following section reviews additional factors that appear most commonly and consistently in lasting changes efforts, whether they involve therapy, a spontaneous or serendipitous event, or an intentional self-help effort. It represents a catalogue of what is known and reasonably agreed upon by most practitioners, regardless of their espoused ideology or theoretical orientation.

Oops

The consensus in the relapse literature is that the best preventive strategy allows people to practice having relapses and then recovering from them. The problem in sustaining change is *not* in having setbacks, but in interpreting them as "failures" rather than inevitable bumps in the road. People can become demoralized and give up when they believe they are facing failure instead of a few temporary obstacles. Note that the important word in the sentence above is "believe." How people interpret and respond to a temporary lapse determines what they will do after it occurs.

James decided to start exercising regularly at the suggestion of his physician who was concerned about his high blood pressure and family history of heart disease. Compulsive by nature, James set up a program in which he would work out at the gym or on his new exercycle for 20 minutes every day. No exceptions or excuses were to be permitted. While his commitment was laudable, James also set himself up for failure the first time he couldn't maintain his daily regimen. It happened almost 3 weeks (19 consecutive days) into his program when a delayed flight made it impossible for him to work out before he had to be at an important meeting. James was so unprepared for this 1-day lapse that his morale suffered a huge blow. If, instead of planning a rigid agenda, he had built in a margin for error, or even forced himself to skip a day for practice, a single lapse would not have been so devastating.

This represents a critical transition point in James' change effort. He may become discouraged enough to cease his health program altogether, or he may redouble his efforts to get back on track the next day. Hopefully, he will also learn an important lesson about planning for unanticipated circumstances that are beyond his control.

Feeling Lost

Those whose lives have been changed forever by a memorable trip commonly report that they encountered some adversity and managed to survive. They often tend to romanticize and minimize experiences that were essentially pretty miserable, as evidenced by many travel stories. The telling of the story may make the trip sound like it was so fun and exciting, but during the events, the participants were often miserable and terrified.

A typical travel story, guaranteed to get lots of laughs, is one in which someone describes how he or she ended up lost in some God-forsaken place. In interviews I conducted for a book on transformative travel (Kottler, 1997), again and again people mentioned that encountering some major challenge they had to overcome most often changed their lives forever. This may have involved getting lost in a strange city, having their luggage stolen, or being caught in the eye of a hurricane. In each case, if they survived with their health and dignity intact, it is highly likely that the story of their escapade became the greatest souvenir of their trip.

In explaining her attraction to adventure-based travel, Hall (1999) explains that it is the source of her courage: "Partly to reclaim my independence, and partly to give my preteen children a better role model, I began timidly venturing out with friends." This progressed eventually to full-fledged treks in Tibet, crossing precipices on rope ladders that were so terrifying even the horses had to be blind-folded."

"Since then," she says, "I've traveled alone to Australia, India, and Nepal—all impossible dreams. I haven't overcome my fears so much as learned to cope with them."

Most people return from an exotic adventure claiming that they are different and, indeed, they are transformed—for a few days or weeks anyway. What made it possible for this world traveller to maintain her commitment was the willingness to apply what she learned on the road to her daily life.

People also report a feeling of unbridled freedom during transformative trips. We can be whomever we choose and nobody else knows it isn't the real us. Free from conventional routines and schedules, we can give ourselves permission to discover unknown parts of the world and of ourselves.

It is only when we return from such a trip that the real work begins. Nobody really understands what we've gone through; they get tired of listening to our stories. The same things we left behind are now in our path once again. Unless we can hold onto what we learned, before long, all we have left are a few photographs and a credit card bill.

It often seems the case that we have to get lost in order to be found. This was quite literally the case for a mountain climber who was left for dead on Mt. Everest. Beck Weathers was part of the doomed 1996 team that was caught in the worst climbing disaster in Everest history. A Texas pathologist who was known to be selfish, self-centered, dogmatic, and neglectful of his family, he was not a very happy man. He was prone to depression, social isolation, and was about to give up on his marriage.

In his book on his death, rebirth, and redemption, Weathers (2000) describes the horror of being left to die in the snow and spending the better part of a day exposed to the elements in below zero temperatures without shelter or even proper clothing. He was eventually revived and brought back to life, but he lost both his hands and nose to frostbite in the process. Needless to say, he returned home a changed man, unable any longer to do the two things he loved most: climb mountains and practice medicine.

It is not surprising that Weathers experienced a quantum change as a result of this trauma and having been literally brought back to life. What is interesting, though, is that even 8 years later, he has been able to maintain the personality transformation by redefining himself and teaching himself to give and receive love (Fimrite, 2000).

Discontent

Most people don't change unless they have to. They don't walk out of a marriage, quit a job, or end a friendship just because it was mildly unsatisfying; they usually feel miserable with the way things are. They change not because they *want* to, but because they *have* to.

Such discontent is often crystallized in a single event or a series of focal incidents (Baumeister, 1994). Problems may have been building over time, but people often report that dissatisfaction is intensified, or at least brought to attention in a way that it can no longer be ignored, as a result of some (often minor) event.

Some theorists, including Haley (1984), have made the provocative point that the object of all therapy is to make clients hate the process so much they will cure themselves in order to escape the distasteful activities. Most therapists would agree that our jobs involve, to some extent, helping clients face things in their lives they would prefer to avoid or ignore. Often this involves confrontation, provocation, challenging, and other interventions that are designed specifically to increase discontent with the dysfunctional status quo. The most effective therapy can sometimes be quite an unpleasant experience for all parties involved. Even when the therapeutic relationship itself proceeds in a reasonably smooth manner, a number of aspects of the client's life are thrown into turmoil as a result of experimenting with new ways of being and behaving.

Altered States

Therapy is a kind of hypnotic process in which people become hyper-suggestible. This must be the case, because almost nobody (including my family and friends) listens to me much in my "civilian" role, but once I am wearing my professor, therapist, or author hat people actually take notes on what I say.

Therapy is a powerful medium for change because clients give us permission to influence them. They make themselves open and accessible in ways they would not ordinarily consider. Even the so-called resistant ones tell us secrets and listen to feedback they would avoid in any other context.

We arrange the setting for our work with the same care that any stage director manages a dramatic play. If we are to win a client's trust so that he or she will listen and be influenced by our incantations, then we must create a nurturing atmosphere that is conducive to meeting those objectives.

When the door to my office shuts, and a client first takes a seat, I can feel myself go into a trance state, taking the client along with me. All of a sudden, I no longer notice extraneous noises outside the window or door. I am no longer hungry, tired, or worried about something in my own life. I see and hear things in the room that would ordinarily escape my attention. My antennae are quivering with exquisite sensitivity, picking up subtle cues in the client's behavior. I feel clear, focused, and with intense and total concentration. If this is not an altered state of consciousness, I don't know what else would qualify.

Clients sit across from us in their own fugue states. They look at us with eager eyes and almost a glazed look, taking in the morsels of wisdom that we offer. We use our own eyes to draw them in. We use our hypnotic voices to soothe and relax them, then persuade them to adopt alternative ways of looking at things. Remarkably, in this altered state, clients not only listen to us, but act on what they hear. The challenge, as always, is to extend the effects of the encounter.

Hope

One specific way we attempt to "hypnotize" clients is by promoting positive expectations for the work that we do. This placebo effect is extremely important, given the degree to which people's expectations for outcomes are clearly related to subsequent results (Frank & Frank, 1991; Lambert, 1992; Snyder, Michael, & Cheavens, 1999).

In order for people to feel hopeful, two conditions have to be met:

1. There must be some workable plan to reach desired goals.
2. There must be a belief that the opportunity and resources exist to follow through on this plan.

In both cases, the emphasis is on the individual's internal thinking and ability to envision a future in which objectives have been obtained. When such hope is not already present, an important part of our job is to "sell" clients on the possibilities for future deliverance. Obviously, consumers are far more open and amenable to what we offer if they are in the sort of hyper-suggestible state described earlier.

Catharsis

Freud and the psychoanalysts aren't the only ones who recognize the value of allowing people to tell their stories. Almost every theory now in practice makes provisions for clients to express themselves fully and to share their narratives in a way that they feel heard and understood. Of course, catharsis alone is often not enough, but it is also unusual to skip this step altogether.

Therapists might identify their clever techniques and powerful interventions as mattering most to clients, but when clients are asked the same question, they often mention more human, relationship variables (Hubble, Duncan, & Miller, 1999). If we do nothing else for people, sometimes having the opportunity to tell their stories is what they recall years later as being significant.

Clinicians structure the catharsis process according to their own style and beliefs about what matters most in their work. Regardless of how clients are invited to talk about their lives and concerns, disclosing their most personal stories and having the audience listen with attentiveness,

respect, and without judgement is a wonderfully freeing process. Whatever else happens afterwards is viewed by some as icing on the cake.

Emotional Arousal

Just as Freud was wrong about catharsis (and its' deeper exploration)
being enough for people to come to terms with their troubles, Carl Rogers
was mistaken in believing that accessing and expressing feelings can
complete the job. Contrary to what the humanists once proposed, stirring
up feelings for their own sake is generally not all that helpful unless this
process leads to some sort of resolution of the emotional activation and
to some constructive action (Greenberg & Safran, 1987; Greenberg, Rice,
& Elliot, 1993).

Unless one is aware of the feelings and acknowledges them, it is difficult to do much to work through them (Greenberg & Rhodes, 1991).
Thus much of what occurs in sessions is emotionally charged, tearful,
and involves intense and dramatic displays of feeling. Various therapists
may work with this material in widely diverse ways that lead to the same
objective: greater degrees of self-respect, self-efficacy, and self-awareness
for their clients.

"I'm just so angry about this situation," a client says with a reddened
face." As he gets himself more worked up, he finally sighs out loud in a
way to suggest that he has reached his limit. "It's just so unfair the way
they've treated me. I just can't get it out of my head."

Faced with this fairly emotionally-laden statement, a dozen therapists
might respond in at least as many ways. Some might stay with the
feelings, encouraging the client to go deeper into the sense of helplessness
he feels. Others might acknowledge what was communicated, but then
lead the discussion to a host of other areas—the underlying thinking, the
specific interactions with the antagonists, the metaphors expressed in this
issue, the patterns from the past that are being replayed in the present
struggle, and so on. Regardless of where such a conversation would go
next, most practitioners would take time to help the client express what
is going on inside and then help him or her come to terms with these
strong feelings in order to move on to more productive areas.

Relationship for Support and Leverage

Most agree that the therapeutic relationship is critical to change efforts,
although there is considerable debate about the best form this alliance

should take. It can be constructed with the therapist in the role of teacher, coach, consultant, parent figure, priest-confessor, expert, or trainer. It can be an intimate, authentic engagement between two people sharing their innermost reactions or it can be a fairly businesslike arrangement. Depending on the client's needs and presenting problems, the relationship can be used therapeutically in a number of different ways:

- As a diagnostic aid for assessing how clients behave.
- As a form of interpersonal engagement to create a human bond of trust and intimacy.
- As a way to complete unfinished business from the past in the form of resolving transferences.
- As a medium for social influence to persuade clients to do things that are good for them.
- As a collaboration to solve problems and generate alternative courses of action.
- As a personal support system during difficult times.
- As a means for creating a template for new ways of interacting in the future.
- As a vehicle for practicing enforcing boundaries.
- As an authentic engagement of people in a safe, secure environment.
- As an environment for creating alternative realities.
- As a structure for promoting constructive risk taking.
- As a vehicle for helping people to face and confront fears.

Many other universal features of change are not only present in the distinctly human connection between clients and therapists, but infused in every facet of therapeutic interventions. The relationship just happens to be the glue that holds everything together and increases the probability that clients will comply with treatment efforts and continue their progress afterwards.

The number of different forms this helping relationship can take, depending on the client's needs, the therapist's preferences, and the conegotiated alliance between them is truly remarkable. Some practitioners may appear nurturing while others come across as very businesslike or down-to-earth. Just as vast are the variations that one clinician exhibits with all his or her clients. He or she may vary the kinds of boundaries enforced, the amount of self revealed, the pace and rhythm of the conversations, and the level of openness. It could even be said that every relationship we build with a client is unique and quite unlike any other we have structured previously. Yet what they all have in common is a level of trust and intimacy that makes it possible to cover new ground.

Major Demolition

So many forms of change, whether in the context of formal therapy or elsewhere, involve an explosion of sorts in which the status quo is shaken up considerably. Clients often feel stuck, immobilized, and unable to pull themselves out of despair, hopelessness, or entrenched patterns.

Therapists function as demolition experts in many different ways. We use confrontation to point out discrepancies between what clients are saying and what they are doing, and between what they are saying now and what they said earlier. We promote insights designed to bring attention to facets of life that have been ignored. We dismantle defenses that, while protective, are also insulating. We use any leverage and influence within our power to get people to complete therapeutic tasks. Most of all, we shake things up in our clients' world to the point at which they no longer have a choice about remaining stuck; moving forward is the only choice.

Task Facilitation

Problem solving, strategic, and brief therapies are not the only ones that employ therapeutic tasks. Indeed, cognitive-behavioral and other abbreviated therapies also make considerable use of homework as the main focus of treatment. Nowadays almost all therapists design activities or assignments that allow clients to practice what they are learning in sessions.

If the goal from the outset is to help clients not only make changes, but make them stick, then therapists must devise ways to help them apply new skills where it matters most—in their everyday lives. Once clients become accustomed to being expected to come up with good things they can start practicing more in their lives, they get into the habit of doing so long after therapy ends.

Behaviorists have proposed and supported empirically that this variable may best predict future generalization of outcomes to other situations. Rehearsal and practice, first in simulated situations and then in real-life predicaments, equip people to transfer learning from what was presented in sessions to what is required in the outside world.

It is one thing to talk about one's troubles, but quite another to take what is realized or learned and use it during times of need. A woman in a group session was complaining about the lack of available men for her to date. At almost every meeting, she brought up this theme and continued to externalize her problems, blaming others for her predicament and feeling lonely and without intimate relationships. Finally, one of the other group members confronted her directly by suggesting that the problem had little to do with the prospects available and everything to do with her own behavior, which made her so inaccessible. "I would never approach you," he confessed. "Even if I wanted to know you, you make yourself so threatening, I'd run in the other direction."

"What do you mean?" she pressed him for specifics. The other group members had no difficulty providing numerous examples of these behaviors, including rarely maintaining eye contact, making herself as unattractive as possible, scaring people away, and cutting off interactions before they had a chance to develop.

As the leader of the group, I kept wracking my brain to think of a way we could take what we were talking about "outside." Although she knew exactly what we were talking about, I was skeptical that the insight would last very long. She had been through this many times before, not only in our group but in many other forms of therapy.

Reasoning that she needed to transfer the talk into action, I instructed her to pick the person in the group she trusted most to be a source of support. She selected another single woman with whom she had shared confidences. "Okay," I said with more confidence then I felt, looking around the group for help. "What task can we come up with that would help her to take a small step in the right direction of reaching out more to men rather than closing them out?" After batting around a few ideas, the group decided that she should walk around the campus with her partner. She was not allowed to return to the group until she made eye contact with at least five different men for at least several seconds. She was not to speak to them, or engage them in any way, but only look at them instead of looking away, as was her usual pattern. It didn't take them more than 15 minutes to complete the task and come back with a look of victory on their faces. This became the beginning of a series of sequential steps she was to continue over the next several months, each of which was designed to change her interaction style forever.

One need not be behaviorally inclined in order to incorporate similar structured tasks into therapy sessions. Most therapists end sessions by asking clients what they intend to do during the time before the next meeting. This holds them accountable, but also introduces the idea that lasting change occurs only with consistent practice.

Creation of New Meaning

All forms of therapy help clients to replace their perceptions of present reality with alternatives that are more useful, self-enhancing, and empowering. Like many of these universal features of therapeutic change, this task is approached by clinicians in many different ways. Cognitive therapists might dispute irrational beliefs. Existential practitioners might encourage looking at underlying issues of angst, meaninglessness, and personal responsibility. Narrative therapists might help people re-author their life stories. Each theory has its own unique operating style, but all have a similar long-range goal: to co-construct with clients a different vision of who they are, where they came from, and where they are going.

It is a mystery as to why some ideas seem to stick in people's heads and others don't. Thinking back on our own past, perhaps the most vivid memories from childhood, it seems that the images that remain instantly retrievable are often fairly ordinary events—sitting on the front porch watching cars go by, eating cotton candy at the fair, or wrestling with one's father on the floor. A million other events and experiences that were considered important at the time are forever forgotten, but apparently random memories remain intact.

So it is with therapy. We are in the business of producing memorable experiences, the kind that stick around for a very long time. Not only must we present brilliant ideas or useful interventions, but they have to remain embedded in a client's mind so they can be retrieved as needed. How frustrating it is to have a startlingly potent session, in which a major new way of looking at things is explored, only to discover the next week that the client can no longer recall what was discussed. So it isn't enough to co-create novel perceptions or coauthor alternative narratives unless the product is personally meaningful enough to truly penetrate the client at a core level. This is much easier said then done.

☐ The Universal Ingredients in Action

The discussion of how and why change occurs has thus far been fairly conceptual. This section looks at the ways these universal features of change operate in a common change scenario: someone trying to lose weight, and most importantly, who is interested in keeping the weight off.

Why Diets Don't Work

"I estimate that I've lost close to 1,000 pounds in my life."

This is a pretty dramatic statement from a woman who doesn't look like she weighs more than 130 pounds, maximum. What she means, though, is that she has been on yo-yo diets her whole life: dropping 10 pounds on the Pritikin diet, then gaining back 15 pounds; losing that 15 pounds at Weight Watchers, then gaining that back and more; drinking only diet milkshakes and getting wheatgrass enemas to lose that 20 pounds, only to see the progress disappear after a few months; staying at a "fat farm" for 2 weeks and reducing two whole sizes, then bloating right up again after resuming her normal routine.

During the course of the past decade, she has tried every diet imaginable, most of them under the direction of various physicians and therapists. She has explored fears of intimacy, distorted body image, repressed memories of possible abuse, negative thinking, and poor self-esteem. She has perfect insight into her problems. At one point, she tried to reframe her predicament from being fat to just "full-bodied." "But the truth is," she says, "I *am* fat, and I'm tired of these damned diets."

As this example illustrates, it is easy to lose weight; the hard part is keeping it off. Diets often don't work because they require people to change their eating habits in unnatural ways that are virtually impossible to maintain after the program is over. They ignore what is known about how lasting change takes place, instead going for the short-term, temporary gain. The hard part about weight loss isn't just dropping excess pounds, but maintaining the changes over time once the diet is over. That's why "diet" is even an inappropriate word to use since it implies a temporary change in eating habits.

Using weight loss as one example of how the preceding features of change might be applied, several specific steps would be involved in sensible therapeutic program. This same process could easily be applied to any other presenting problem. The premise of such a change effort would be very simple: Rather than going on a diet, which involves little transfer of learning, the object is to change the way one thinks and acts with regard to eating. This would involve a major, permanent shift in the perception of self, as well as of the meaning of food.

Step 1: Educate Yourself About Sensible Eating Habits

As with other lifestyle change efforts, including substance abuse and smoking cessation treatment, it helps considerably to have accurate information about the nature of the phenomenon. This would include the basics about metabolism and digestion, the various food groups, and what is already known to be most and least effective in helping people achieve healthy eating habits.

In a desperate attempt to drop a few pounds, one man regularly did warm-up exercises, ran three miles, and then sat in the steam room for a half hour. Afterwards, he would quench his thirst with a fruit smoothie, which had roughly double the amount of calories that he had just burned off. Many people do not have good information and sound strategies for reaching their goals.

Unfortunately, such information is not sufficient for a change effort to last. Most smokers know what the habit is doing to their lungs, heart, and lifespan, but that knowledge doesn't have a major impact on behavior. Nevertheless, the absence of solid information can certainly make any change effort futile.

Step 2: Eat Anything You Want, Whenever You Want, and Still Lose Weight

I know, it sounds too good to be true. The problem with diets, however, is that people deprive themselves, temporarily, of the foods they crave most. They manage to stay away from potato chips or chocolate chip cookies for a few weeks or months, but find themselves dreaming about them and craving them constantly. They practice diligent self-restrictions—eating dry baked potatoes, drinking lemon in hot water, avoiding any sugars or starches—but because they are unable and unwilling to continue this practice for the rest of their lives, they eventually return to previous bad habits. Thus, any lasting change effort, with the exception of one in which incremental behaviors are "chained" to an ultimate goal, must involve alterations in behavior that can be maintained not just for a few weeks, but for the rest of one's life.

An alternative is to *not* give up the foods one enjoys the most, but rather to eat them in controlled, intentional, and modest amounts. Ice cream, corn chips, and chocolate mousse are not the culprits: how much of them one consumes is what matters.

This sample plan allows people to eat anything they want, without restrictions within reason and without gross deprivation of their favorite foods.

So, what's the catch?

Step 3: Eat Only What You Plan Ahead of Time

The bad news is that a person is no longer permitted to eat spontaneously and impulsively. Anything can be eaten as long as what that will be, when that will be, and how much that will be is planned ahead of time. No excuses are accepted. Few, if any, substitutions are permitted. Such planning prevents unforeseen circumstances from leading to possible relapse. This process thus makes the person totally responsible for what goes in the mouth and trains him or her to behave differently.

Of course, this reduces one's spontaneity and freedom. A person can't decide at the last minute, or even a few hours ahead of time, that he or she feels like eating a particular meal or food item because all food choices are governed by a preplanned schedule. This requires a very high degree of self-control—serious, *sustained* self-control over the course of one's lifetime.

Step 4: Plan Menus One Day in Advance

The plan is simple. Each morning (or preferably the night before) people plan exactly what they will eat the next day, how much they will eat, and when they will eat it. Anything on their menus can be placed on this list. Initially, the object is not to lose weight or change anything about one's eating habits; that comes later. For now, the goal is to become accustomed to planning the day's food consumption and sticking with the program no matter what. This means getting into the habit of making daily commitments to following the program and keeping that promise. The most important part of this, or any attempt to permanently reprogram behavior, is the idea of "getting into the habit" in order to make a strategy as automatic as brushing one's teeth.

The rules allow for items on the list to be skipped, but no additions are permitted. If someone *might* want a Snickers bar in the middle of the afternoon, he or she should put it on the list. If John thinks he *may* meet a friend for a latte, he should put it on the list. If Alice could end up at a bar later that evening and have a few drinks, she should put them on the list, just in case. But if they didn't think to put something down, they can't have it, no matter what. Remember, this is an exercise in self-control and commitment that is to be maintained through the course of one's life.

This structured method can be very annoying, especially when someone receives sudden invitations or encounters spontaneous opportunities for socializing. It doesn't take long, however, to get very good at anticipating what may unfold. This is, of course, a metaphor not only for losing weight but for making any relatively permanent change. The key to preventing relapses is being able to anticipate threatening or risky situations so that they can be avoided or circumvented.

Step 5: Anticipate Problems

The best excuse goes something like this: "How was I supposed to know they were having this party?" In other words, unanticipated things happen in life, many of which involve food.

The areas in which people are most likely to experience trouble include:

- *Unplanned social events.* "When I got to the office, they were having a birthday party for one of the secretaries. It would have been rude not to have some cake."
- *Peer pressure.* "I brought my sandwich and fruit to the staff lounge for lunch, but everyone was going out for lunch to that new French restaurant. What could I do?"
- *Gifts.* "I don't ordinarily eat this kind of stuff, but they gave me this huge jar of jelly beans. I couldn't exactly just throw it out."
- *Schedule changes.* "When I made up my menu for the day I thought we'd be eating home, but my husband surprised me by taking us out."

Smart people come up with brilliant excuses. The important thing about this whole program is getting into the habit of anticipating unforeseen events and teaching others in one's life to take this into consideration. This involves sometimes feeling awkward and uncomfortable, but also feeling pride in keeping commitments.

Step 6: Review How Things Are Going

After the first week is over, the person should review the menus that were constructed and circle any areas of particular difficulty sticking with promises. If the person was able to maintain control for 7 days in a row (with only one or two minor adjustments), he or she can go on to the next step. Otherwise, continue the plan as described until the person can complete 7 days in a row of eating what was planned ahead of time.

Step 7: Make Changes in Eating Patterns

Under no circumstances should someone initiate a diet at this point. A day's menu should include well-balanced meals as well as favorite "comfort" foods. For me, these include graham crackers dunked in milk, frozen yogurt, and a bowl of corn flakes with a banana. For others, they might include something else. It is important not to deprive oneself of foods that matter or that might be craved, but to work toward reducing the portions consumed.

During this stage, minor adjustments in quantity and quality of foods are made slowly and gradually. Once again, eating favorite foods in controlled doses, rather than depriving oneself, is the key. Someone who loves chicken fried steak or malted milk balls should continue to eat them, but plan to eat a little less than usual. Someone who ordinarily eats a hamburger, large fries, and a large coke for lunch, should plan to leave at least one bite of the sandwich, pass up three of the fries, and instead drink a diet coke or a medium regular coke. This is not dramatic progress, and that is the point. The individual is making gradual, incremental, easy changes and is sticking with a plan no matter what.

Intentionally throwing away a sandwich with one bite left provides a world of confidence to someone who has been controlled by food his or her whole life. Learning to slow down the pace of eating, savoring each bite more, and resting between swallows are also helpful. Again, keep in mind that the object here is not to lose weight—that will come eventually—but to change behaviors in ways that can be maintained forever.

Step 8: Keep the Progress Going

This stage involves slowly tinkering with the system until the person has planned well-balanced, sensible, healthy meals and snacks throughout the day. After a period of months, it will no longer be necessary to write everything down. Once there is an ongoing pattern of keeping self-commitments, the menus can be created internally.

☐ Return to Stability

Dieting is an example of an ineffective change strategy that is known to be susceptible to relapses. The same holds true for the ways people often try to stop any habit. Someone who wants to stop smoking may throw on a nicotine patch or go to see a hypnotist, thinking that's all that is necessary. People are often looking for easy solutions and quick, effortless cures, as we well know.

One of our most difficult tasks, especially in this era of quick cures, is to plan for not only significant, measurable changes, but also enduring effects that stand the test of time. In a culture like ours that is obsessed with quick, easy, and painless solutions, it is even more challenging to structure reasonable and sensible treatments in such a way that our clients will follow through on the hard, sustained work involved.

Clients often don't stick with their best intentions because of their unwillingness to live in a prolonged state of instability. We may be tempted, as therapists, to abandon the universal features that we know are crucial for long-term gains in order to produce the instant results necessary to win a degree of credibility. Financial considerations may also provide us with only three or four sessions in which to make a difference. In order for lasting changes to be attained within such constraints, we must capitalize on those therapeutic ingredients that are most consistently associated with sustained progress.

6

The Process of Lasting Change

There have been several attempts to integrate all that is known about change processes into a unified model, but very few such efforts directed to plotting the mechanisms of permanent changes, that is, those that are sustained over time. In fact, most systematic interventions often end at the point the client walks out of the office for the last time, as if it is assumed that the happy ending will endure.

Since this book is about not so much what brings about change, but what makes it last, we will examine a model that seeks to explain the factors contributing most to relatively permanent effects. This framework can act as a guide for clinicians to not only understand the forces with which they are dealing, but also plan more strategically to help supposed cures endure longer.

In Figure 1, a flow chart summarizes the process by which lasting change occurs. I have included not only concepts from clinical disciplines, but also features from learning theory, brain-based learning, and neurological mechanisms related to memory, retention, and transfer of learning. The model follows a series of thresholds that must be reached, then exceeded, in order for efforts to proceed to the next stage.

☐ The Model in Action

The personal example used in this chapter to illustrate this process model occurred during the time the stages were being constructed. Actually,

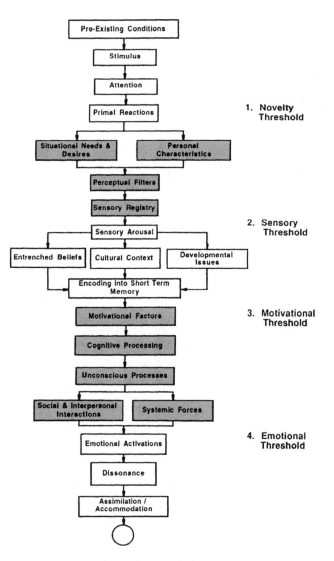

FIGURE 1. Threshold Model of How Changes Last

as is so often the case when we try to describe or explain change, the sequence took place the other way around: This little incident provided a framework by which I could hang the various stages in the process.

According to this model, there is a series of nine thresholds that must be reached, then exceeded, in order for change to move along to the next succeeding stage, eventually cementing its effects. If, for example, some-

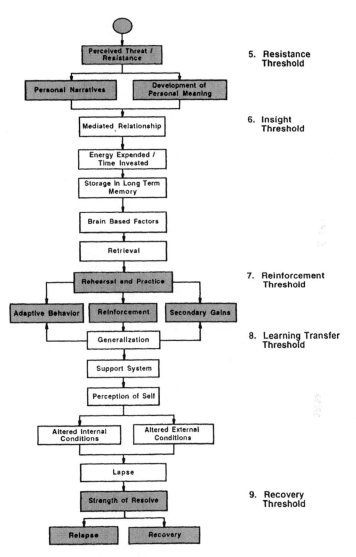

FIGURE 1. (*Continued*)

one experienced a moment of grand insight in which the whole world seemed to tip on its axis, yet the meaning was never generalized beyond the specific incident, then the process would not move any further. Our job as therapists is, therefore, to help our clients proceed through the gates of each threshold and move on to the next level.

The Stimulus

I had just parked my car in the lot by my office. As I made the brief automatic walk to the building, a movement caught my eye. At the corner of a flower bed I saw a small bird—perhaps a sparrow—wiggling in its death throes. It looked mortally wounded.

While I had been thinking about what would unfold during the day, my attention was immediately diverted to this novel stimulus. I stood frozen in midstride, both riveted and revolted by the flopping movements of this suffering bird.

Novelty Threshold

My first reaction, at least the one of which I was initially aware, was a startled response. A dying bird was not something I saw every day; in fact, it was so unusual that I felt some anxiety and apprehension until I recognized that I wasn't in danger.

This was the first threshold that would determine whether this experience would become memorable and transformative for me or not. There are many times in any given day that I encounter strange stimuli but don't give them a second's consideration. There was something about this event that grabbed me on a primal level.

Personal Characteristics and Filters

I am a photographer, so I'm used to staring at the ground, looking for colors, shapes, shadows, and light. I have a few other personal characteristics that might be relevant: a tendency, perhaps typical of many therapists, to reflect on things I encounter; and a personal style that is critical. At this moment in time, I was neither hungry nor fatigued. My senses were heightened and sharp at the beginning of the day, almost oversensitive and raw.

I did not see just a dying bird lying there on the ground. Through my perceptual filters, at that moment I saw a fellow being drawing its last breaths on this planet. This image had particular power for me given that this was my 48th birthday.

Sensory Arousal

As my eyes, ears, and other senses took in this dying bird, I was impacted at a profound level. Even though I couldn't name what I was experiencing, I felt my heart speed up and a great sadness overcome me.

The sensory threshold was registered and aroused to the point that this relatively insignificant event activated considerable cognitive and physiological activity. I could not only feel my heart thumping, but I could feel moisture pooling in my eyes.

I have some particular ideas and associations about what death means—for both birds and myself. Many of these attitudes, shaped by my unique culture and developmental functioning, color what I see and interpret about the world. Whatever was going inside me, it was the kind of thing that had a hold on me. It would be safe to say that this experience became encoded into my short-term memory. Whatever else might occur, I would not forget that incident a few minutes later. Its image would haunt me later. The only question was how long the influence would last.

Cognitive Processing

Free will now comes into the picture. I could have walked onward, refocused my attention on what was waiting for me in the building, and put this brief encounter with a dying bird in temporary storage, where all other such intermittent experiences go. Instead, I felt highly motivated to take things further, to make sense of what just happened, or at the very least, to give myself permission to explore what it meant to me.

During the cognitive processing stage, a number of parallel processes come into play. First, I felt flooded by images from the past—of the time as a child when I held a dead bird in my hand and was surprised how light it felt; the time when I shot at a bird with a rifle and knocked it off a branch; then connections to death, funerals, and my mother's last days before cancer killed her; and finally, most disturbing of all, an uninvited image of my own death in which I was lying on the ground with people stepping over me.

In the flash of a second I recalled visiting Las Vegas a decade earlier for a job interview. I got up early one morning and went for a walk on the Strip. While strolling along in front of the erupting volcano at the Mirage hotel, I was struck by the gaudy sculptures of Roman gods guarding Caesars Palace ahead. Distracted by the sights, I was surprised to bump into something rather soft and pliable with my sandaled foot. I looked down at the ground, and there staring up at me from the sidewalk was the body of well-dressed man who was obviously dead. I had never seen a dead body up close before so I was both shocked, then fascinated, with his open eyes and unnatural, twisted position on the ground. Apparently, he collapsed after suffering a heart attack.

What amazed me most about this whole episode was that nobody else seemed to notice or care that there was a dead may lying on the pavement. People must have been passing by him, even stepping over him, for several minutes, maybe even longer. I knew that in Las Vegas people could be single-minded in their pursuit of riches, but could they really not notice a body on the ground? Was this man's life worth so little that he could keel over and nobody would care? And, of more concern to me at the time, what if this happened to me?

In addition to this potent imagery from the past, I was also processing automatically, and perhaps unconsciously, other information that had been taken in (and was still coming in). My cultural background, language, and prior experiences were also governing the ways I interpreted the data.

Systemic Context

Except for a few other pedestrians who passed by, perhaps staring at me curiously as I stood riveted to my spot on the walkway staring at this bird, I was essentially alone while experiencing this stimulus. Most events occur within an interpersonal and systemic context. At that moment I had not yet interacted with other people, but if this event were to become a significant impetus for permanent change in my life, it would surely become part of my interactions with others. I was aware only that my emotions were raw and exposed. I could feel more tears of sadness well up in my eyes. I started to feel depressed.

Emotional Activation

This threshold of emotional activation further ensured that this "bird episode" would loom even larger in my consciousness. Unlikely to be quickly forgotten, it seemed destined for relocation to more permanent memory storage. First, however, I could feel dissonance starting to build. I felt uncomfortable with this state of temporary disorientation, which activated increased motivation to do something with this experience—get rid of it, bury it, disguise it, or if nothing else works, reduce the discomfort by making needed adjustments.

While being emotionally upset is not a pretty or welcome condition, it often appears necessary for lasting change. It gets our attention in a way that nothing else can. It serves as a kind of memory anchor that makes for easy retrieval. And it also acts as a powerful incentive to reduce the pain.

Knowing that emotional upheaval can be such an effective trigger and motivator, therapists are usually comfortable being in the presence of others who are emotionally distraught. Indeed, a box of tissues remains one of the main props in any therapist's office. And rather than being unduly disturbed when a client becomes angry, sad, or elated, we often view such states as opportunities for real growth to take place (unless the displays are excessive, chronic, or totally uncontrolled).

Assimilation

The process of change is often romanticized, as if it were fun, when it really involves an extraordinary amount of work and energy. In this case, I wasn't looking for changes in my life, but neither could I pretend that they weren't happening. I wanted to catalogue this experience in my existing storage bins—assimilation, it is called by Piaget. Since I couldn't find anywhere appropriate, it was necessary to make some accommodations and to create a new schema.

Resistance Threshold

Another threshold has now been reached, one related to the resistance and perceived threats I was experiencing as a result of this episode. If I found this all to be too much to handle, I would shut down and activate defense mechanisms in order to deny or disown the incident. In fact, the perceived threat was high for me at that moment. For the purposes of this illustration, I am making it appear as if the stages in the process were continuous and occurred within a matter of minutes. Actually, thus far, this was the case. But to take things further, there would be an intermission.

Indwelling and Personal Meaning

I put the bird, with its accompanying associations, out of my mind for awhile, leaving them to rumble around inside me while I began the business of my day. At various times during the next hours as I met with students, responded to correspondence, and talked with colleagues, I felt haunted. It was during a boring committee meeting that I doodled on a pad of paper and continued processing what had happened earlier. I was fully immersed in what constructionists like to call "meaning making." I was creating a personal narrative and constructing a story that captured the essence of my experience. Since none of these stages are actually discrete, separate processes, it was at that point that I recycled many of the cognitive activities that began earlier. What seemed especially real for me was my identification with the dying bird and the experience of feeling my own mortality.

As I sat in the meeting and listened to people argue about some issue, I remembered how earlier I had been in such a hurry to complete several errands. I rushed to the drug store to get some eye drops, then became impatient with the cashier who couldn't seem to work the register. I dropped the item I wanted on the counter and walked out of the store in a huff, only to drive over the speed limit to my next errand, and to the next as well. What didn't strike me until that moment, and it struck me *hard*, was that I couldn't think of a single reason why I was in such a hurry. I had no place else to go. I realized that this was the way I lived my life: impatient, always in a hurry to get somewhere, forgetting to smell the flowers that would one day grow over me just like they were swallowing that poor bird.

I had gone as far as I could with my narrative at that point; besides, the meeting was over. If it wasn't clear to me at the time, then some other inner wisdom realized that I needed to talk to someone about what was troubling me. I couldn't work this out on my own, and I couldn't leave it alone.

Mediated Relationship

I could have consulted a therapist and probably would have profited from professional help. Instead, however, I decided to talk a friend who happened to be available. Although a helping relationship is certainly not necessary for transformative change and integration of learning, it sure makes things easier. In this case, hearing myself talking out loud about the issues may have been more useful (right then) than anything this person said or did. Of course, the support and feedback he offered made it more likely that I would allow the process to continue.

Like anyone straddling the thresholds between resistance and enlightenment, I was feeling raw and vulnerable. Although little in this conversation with my friend clarified matters significantly, the whole idea of feeling supported in that moment was enough to calm me down so I could think straighter.

Commitment and Rehearsal

So far, there had been a minimal but sufficient investment of time and energy into the process for this experience to have been transferred into relatively long-term (or perhaps medium-term) storage. The bird, and all it represented to me, was now living inside me, easily accessible upon demand. Apparently, this stimulus, with its corresponding reactions, made such an impression that I then began to devote more time and energy to making sense of this encounter. More than that, however, I began to incorporate the lessons into my conversations and interactions with others. I began to ask people about how they were dealing with the aging process. I noticed that in my therapy sessions, supervision encounters, and classes, I found ways to bring up existential issues related to death.

Reinforcement Threshold

I had now reached another threshold, after which it would be determined whether I would soon forget about all this depressing stuff and move on, or whether it would stick with me over time. We know well from reinforcement theory that behaviors that become rewarding are likely to be continued while those that provide few benefits tend to become extinguished.

There are, of course, several ways that behaviors become rewarding. Most obviously, if behavior is adaptive, that is, if it gets our needs met and produces the effects we like, then we're likely to continue the behavior. In this example, I did find it satisfying to talk to others about my struggle. These discussions created more intimacy in my relationships. I felt less dissonance and discomfort the more I attempted to make sense of what had occurred. There were "secondary" benefits as well, meaning those that were side effects of my behavior. I was enjoying feeling like a martyr. I liked the attention and sympathy I was getting during my struggle. And I especially prized the image of myself as a fearless "truth seeker" who was unafraid of confronting his demons.

Transfer of Learning

Conceivably, the growth and learning that had so far emerged could remain compartmentalized to one small arena. If so, I could still experience a lasting change, but of small magnitude, or even smaller significance. If I let things go at this point, which in fact I did, then I might remember forever what occurred, derive some change from the episode, but not necessarily transform my life, my thinking, or my actions in any appreciable way.

Since the nature of this particular experience was so complex, so interwoven into many facets of my being, I could not pass the transfer of learning threshold that would allow me to generalize the learning to other areas of my life. If I had been ready and so inclined, I could have used this object lesson to make some significant changes in my values, lifestyle, and priorities. That may yet occur.

What was missing for me at that point was a support system that would encourage me to take this to the next level. It was not that my wife, son, friends and colleagues, would not support my efforts; it was more that they were not at a similar place. I felt alone even though I realized, intellectually, that everyone struggles with their mortality and aging.

Maybe it would take something more, perhaps even systematic research on the nature of lasting change, in order for me to experience transformative changes in my essential self. Sure enough, as I talk with people about their most significant, lasting transformations, I continue my own process. The more I read and understand about what makes change last, the more I notice that I take small, progressive steps to incorporate the concepts into my actions.

I revisit, again and again—during dreams, fantasies, journal entries, conversations, and other reflective time—the previous stages in the process. The lessons saturate me more fully. I make a job change. I make lifestyle changes. I alter the ways I spend my time. Now there is no going back; I couldn't change my mind if I wanted to. From the moment that little bird entered my life, until this very second, I continue to make enduring changes.

Naturally, these so-called lasting changes will be influenced by altered internal and external conditions. If I get sick, if I lose income, if someone I love is injured, or if I should see another dying bird, perhaps I will launch myself in a whole new direction.

Recovery Threshold

The story doesn't end here. As I write these words one year later, I find myself still struggling with the same issues. Today I was waiting in line at the post office, frustrated and perturbed because things were proceeding so slowly. "Why can't they run this operation like Federal Express?" I castigated myself for not going there instead. Here it was during peak hours and they had one clerk working to handle the long line. No wonder they had signs around warning customers it was considered a federal crime to take violent action against postal employees.

I stopped for a moment during my internal tirade and consciously stopped my impatient foot from tapping. What was my hurry, I wondered? What was so important that I had to do when I got out of there? How would my life be improved if they had five clerks working or there were no line at all? The value of my moments standing in that line were exactly the same as they would have been if I had been driving home or back at my computer typing away.

I thought back to the bird during this lapse in commitment (another one damn it!) and then increased my resolve to remember the lesson learned. I am now back on track because I recognized the early warning signs of possible relapse and then made needed corrections. This was possible not only because the goal is so important to me but because I have worked to develop the coping skills needed to make such lapses only temporary setbacks rather than a major regression.

Complexity

What makes the phenomenon of lasting change so complex is that it involves so many distinct processes. Sensory awareness and stimulation are the perceptual filters through which the world is experienced. Short-term and long-term memory represent additional layers, as do one's prior history and association with any event. Characterological factors, including personality and interpersonal style, also exert influence.

This isn't just about memory because there are so many examples of people remembering events and even understanding what is happening, but still not acting on what was learned. Consider the example of someone putting a piece of chocolate fudge cake in front of Joe. He remembers its not on his diet. He understands that with his current weight and heart problems its not good for him. He is highly motivated to abstain from food indulgences that are self-destructive. He has changed his patterns of consumption so that he no longer eat desserts. He even likes the new self defined in this manner. Yet this time, he reaches for the cake, almost against his will, as if someone else is borrowing his arm to reach for the temptation. The cognitive activity inside his head, usually so helpful in checking impulsive lapses, fails him now. He stuffs the cake inside his mouth so fast that he isn't aware of thinking about anything at all—just how incredible the sensations are inside his body. Quickly, before guilt takes hold, he grabs another piece, then another.

This example of a change that didn't last (so far anyway), clearly didn't involve a problem in memory, although most of the action was taking place at a sensory level (sight, smell, feel, taste). Let's go back and look at the points at which something else would need to have happened in order for the change effects to have been more enduring.

☐ Preventing Relapses

One attempt to explain the mechanisms by which clients revert to previous levels of dysfunction after they have mastered new adaptive skills is presented in a theory by Laws (1995) who integrated the work of others (Marlatt & Gordon, 1985; Wanigaratne et al, 1990; Pithers, 1991; Wilson, 1992). In Figure 2, the various stages of deterioration are plotted.

☐ The Cure

We begin the story with a supposed cure. A client had originally entered treatment at the request of other family members because of a "bad temper" and "uncontrollable rage" that had been diagnosed as an "explosive personality disorder." In some ways, he quite liked this diagnosis because it let him off the hook. "Shit Doc, if I got one of *those* disorders, what can I do about it? It's like cancer or something, ain't it?"

Over the course of several months, the angry man addressed a number of unresolved issues in his life—the origins of his anger, the behavior patterns that resembled those of his own father, the secondary gains he was enjoying as a result of the behavior, and other insights that helped him to reconceptualize the meaning and consequences of his behavior. His family members also became involved in treatment, exam-

Abstinence
↓
Seemingly Irrelevant Decisions
↓
First Minor Lapse
↓
High Risk Situations
↓
More Severe Lapse
↓
Maladaptive Coping Response
↓
Abstinence Violation Effect
↓
Relapse
↓
Return to Baseline

FIGURE 2. Process of Relapse

ining ways that they were connected to the presenting problems, both as causes and effects. Finally, considerable attention was spent rehearsing difficult situations that might arise and how he would cope with them in ways other than explosive outbursts. He thus learned internally based cognitive self-talk strategies, as well as alternative ways to get his needs met.

At the time treatment ended, he no longer exhibited explosive or angry outbursts. His family was happy. And he too was happy with the outcome. End of story.

The Sequel

One of the most frustrating aspects of our jobs is that our clients often leave—either satisfied or unsatisfied with the outcome—and we never hear what happened to them afterward. We are left to wonder whether the progress they made lasted very long, or whether they reverted to old patterns. We might do our best to initiate follow-up procedures or schedule booster sessions, but as often as not, the clients decide not to participate. So we are left with our own assumptions about how the story might continue.

In this case, the therapist did indeed have his doubts. He never really trusted that this man was being all that open and honest; at times, he seemed to be performing according to what was expected. Nevertheless, the therapist was impressed with the progress he made. He would be dishonest, however, if he said he was taken by surprise when he heard through the grapevine that a few months after the therapy ended the client continued his assaultive and verbally abusive behavior, eventually being arrested in a barfight.

In reconstructing the series of mini-events that led to the man's regression and relapse to previous dysfunctional behavior, the following stages occurred as illustrated in Figure 2.

Abstinence

The client left treatment meeting all the conditions sufficient to qualify for a stable recovery. He had not engaged in abusive behavior or in a single angry outburst for a period of weeks prior to leaving therapy. Both the client and his family reported that he been using alternative strategies quite effectively. He appeared both confident and optimistic that the effects would last and that he could continue the efforts on his own. Nevertheless, a follow-up session was scheduled a month hence just to check on his progress. It was during this appointment that the therapist learned about the progressive fall from grace.

Seemingly Irrelevant Decisions

This stage goes by many different names in the relapse literature, such as "apparently irrelevant decisions" (Marlatt & Gordon, 1985), "seemingly unimportant decisions" (Pithers, 1991), or even simply "setups" (Wanigaratne et al., 1990). Laws (1995) prefers to think of these mini-choices as "irrelevant" because at the time they don't appear to be related to anything very important. They are just tiny, little slips that often go unnoticed that bring the client one small step closer to a more prominent lapse.

In the case of our explosive client, he was at the convenience store picking up a few bottles of ale (the first sign that he was willing to relinquish some control). When the cashier informed him that he could not break up a six-pack in order to buy individual bottles, an argument ensued. The client called the cashier an asshole, threw the bottles on the counter, and walked out of the store. In his mind he had exercised phenomenal control. More accurately, he manifested the beginnings of the same sort of behavior that had repeatedly gotten him into trouble before. Not only did the client not see things that way, but he was thinking to himself that he handled the situation pretty well. "I could've killed the fucker," he related to the therapist, "but I just let it go."

High-Risk Situations

Unfortunately, neither the client nor his family were aware of these beginning rumblings of instability in his behavior. So it didn't concern any of them particularly when bowling season began. In the past, this client often gotten quite drunk and ended up in fights during bowling night out with his friends. By the time he arrived home, he could be quite explosive and abusive with whomever was still awake.

The client actually had no business returning to a toxic environment that could easily provoke previous maladaptive behavior, nor should he have been indulging in alcohol use, which would lower his inhibition levels. Nevertheless, because he viewed himself as perfectly in control, he felt ready to tackle the situation. "Besides," he reported, "I gotta have some fun. And these guys are my friends."

The client actually did remarkably well the first bowling night out. He drank Cokes instead of beers. "Well, I finished one guy's beer as we started to leave, but that didn't count." He didn't get into any major arguments (although he did have a minor skirmish with a guy in the next lane who kept making groaning noises as he released the ball).

We can see now that this client was returning to the same habits and lifestyle that supported and reinforced his explosive behavior in the first place. In the context of his world, his outbursts were highly functional in that they pressured others to give in to him.

Lapse

The client then moved toward his first official setback. High risk situations are those in which tension, social pressure, and conflicts are accompanied by negative emotional arousal. During a family gathering of extended relatives, not the easiest of situations for our angry fellow, he started to argue with an uncle. Not suprisingly, the elderly gentleman was still angry from the last time they tangled. He enjoyed pushing people's buttons in general, and especially those of his nephew who put on such spectacular displays when provoked.

Angry words escalated into shoving one another. Then other family members got involved, they chose sides, and a war began. When the client started screaming to the point that the veins in his neck and forehead started to pulse dangerously, the party quickly ended.

Maladaptive Coping Responses

What started out as a serious lapse became a pattern when the dysfunctional behaviors were repeated. The client tried hard to regain control of himself, and was mostly successful in doing so. But once his temper reappeared on the scene, the incidences of explosiveness became more frequent—from once a week to once a day (but still much less frequent than before treatment).

Abstinence Violation Effect

During this most critical stage, a client decides what to think about this lapse and chooses what to do afterwards. If sufficient work has been done in therapy to prepare for this inevitable lapse, then perhaps the client is able to shrug off the temporary error in judgement and return to previous levels of functioning. If he is really smart, he recognizes that he again has the beginnings of a problem and returns for additional treatment focused on preventing future relapses.

In this case, however, the client started to feel hopeless and despondent. "I'll never be able to get this shit under control," he muttered to himself. "This situation is hopeless."

Of course, he had been taught to practice other kinds of internally based thoughts, like "Just because I make one mistake doesn't mean I have to return to my old self." But in the throes of self-flagellation, whatever thoughts he once rehearsed became lost amid his sense of guilt and frustration. Once he thought to himself, "I guess the therapy crap didn't work after all. I'm right back where I started," he was then well on his way to a full-fledged relapse.

Relapse

When lapses become more frequent, dysfunctional lifestyle is resumed, and the client loses all hope for recovery, then a relapse is officially operating. The thresholds described in the previous model had not been exceeded to the point where learning would endure. There continues to be a steady decline in effectiveness, even though there may be a brief rebound effect that doesn't last very long.

Return to Baseline

This stage brings us back to where things first began. This time, however, there is even less hope and optimism that future treatments will be successful. A therapist attempting to get reinvolved with the case at this point, would certainly face a difficult chore, especially when compared with the earlier situation. That is one reason why it is so important to plan for lasting change in the first place.

In the following chapter, we look more specifically at ways the two models presented can be applied to various clinical situations in which the goal is to produce permanent change.

Conditions That Promote Enduring Change

It sometimes appears that permanent change is almost impossible to achieve given all the impediments, obstacles, challenges, and resistance along the way. Yet looked at from another point of view, change is so natural and inevitable that often all you have to do is go along for the ride and resist the urge to put the brakes on. This is especially the case when people become so desperate that they have very little left to lose. "There is a certain relief in change," noted author Washington Irving (1824/1993), "even though it can be from bad to worse; as I have found travelling in a stage-coach, that it is often a comfort to shift one's position and be bruised in a new place."

This chapter looks at the conditions that most consistently contribute to the natural, progressive, and enduring state of change. We begin with what is known to work best once people have attained a precarious fingerhold on a new position. The focus is on not so much what can be done to climb higher, but rather what is most helpful to stabilize current progress.

Relapse Prevention

The relapse prevention specialty made huge strides when Marlatt and Gordon (1985) attempted to identify the high-risk situations that put people in greatest jeopardy. They then set about training them in skills that are helpful in maintaining progress and resisting temptations, including inoculating clients against the need for immediate gratification and practicing adaptive ways of saying no to coercion by peers. In terms of the models presented in the previous chapter, this would involve exceeding the transfer of learning threshold or recovering from lapses with one's confidence and self-efficacy intact.

Others have since adapted the relapse prevention model from the field of addictions to other populations such as sex offenders (Pithers, 1991). The focus of such training involves helping clients to become more vigilant about mini-decisions they make that draw them closer to a lapse in judgement. For instance, the choice to purchase pornography might be one of those high-risk behaviors that increase the probability that acting out might follow. Rather than waiting for a full-fledged relapse to occur, it is best to recognize and counteract smaller regressions that may signal impending problems.

Primary Conditions

Drawing upon the contributors of research discussed earlier, we can distill the variables most associated with changes that persist in the face of threats, challenges, and lapses to three basic conditions. Just as a pilot reviews a check-off list before he or she begins to rev up engines and begin takeoff procedures, therapists interested in promoting lasting changes should consider these items:

1. *Is there sufficient commitment to maintain continued motivation?* This means that the person must have the will, endurance, and motivation to sustain efforts. If a high level of persistence is not present, work will need to be done to bolster future proactive energy. Of course, the challenging part of this process involves assessing accurately how clients are feeling about future progress because they may deny their doubts or not really know where they stand.

2. *Does the person have the necessary coping skills to do what is needed?* This may involve being assertive, recognizing and avoiding high-risk situations, or internalizing constructive self-talk to counteract temptations. Since lapses and setbacks are predictable and inevitable, the question is not so much when the client will fail, but what will be done when this occurs. Rehearsal, practice, simulations, and programmed lapses and recovery are especially useful when helping clients learn and apply the needed coping skills.

3. *Does the client make sound decisions with respect to using the resources available?* It isn't enough to be highly skilled if the person does

not apply these behaviors and training wisely and consistently. We have all seen clients who know and understand far more than we do about their problems, but still fail to use this knowledge when it counts.

These three main factors cover most of the territory, but they are hardly comprehensive. Each of these variables is connected to several others that will be reviewed in this chapter. If any one of these areas is weak, the others can easily topple as well.

Commitment

This factor is mentioned again because it is probably the single most important ingredient. Just how badly does the client really want to change? More important, once the process has begun and things have stabilized, how motivated is the person to maintain gains?

There are several factors that contribute most to the strength of commitment and resolution:

1. *It must be the client's own decision to change.* It does not work very well, or for very long, if the person is going through the motions in therapy to please others.
2. *People must see clear reasons and consequences for making changes.* Until they can articulate, in their own words, exactly what they are doing and why they are doing it, change efforts will likely remain weak.
3. *External incentives must be in place to reinforce decisions.* This is the important support system that we have discussed before (and will again).
4. *Public declaration of commitment is useful.* It always helps to verbalize to others what will be done. It is much harder to back down and regress once someone is on public record.
5. *Temptations must be avoided whenever possible.* This may seem rather obvious but it is amazing how often clients willingly subject themselves to the same situations that got them into trouble. Overconfidence can be the greatest enemy to lasting change.
6. *Coping skills are necessary to maintain resolve in the face of temptations.* This is the relapse prevention material that has been described.
7. *There must be opportunities to practice skills in a safe environment.* This includes role playing and rehearsal in sessions, as well as structured homework outside therapy.
8. *Self-inoculation cognitions must be readily available.* This involves teaching clients constructive ways to talk to themselves when faced with threatening or difficult predicaments.

When commitment is high and the client is prepared in the preceding ways, high-risk situations that cannot be avoided can be managed more effectively.

High-Risk Situations

It certainly helps to prepare for the worst. Relapses and backsliding are not only possible, but probable, especially when one is faced with situations that have been the most challenging in the past. A problem drinker is given a bottle of vodka for a present. An ex-smoker works in a department in which her two closest friends smoke cigarettes continuously. A recent divorcee knows that she is going to be seeing her ex-husband at a social function in the next week. A man with chronic shyness has been invited to the type of social gathering he would ordinarily avoid. A grieving widow is approaching the first anniversary of her husband's death. A therapist has a scheduled session with someone who has consistently gotten underneath her skin in the past.

The process of identifying and targeting high-risk situations represents a significant step toward preventing a serious relapse. A behavioral model (Spiegler & Guevremont, 1998) recommends taking the following steps in order to promote greater durability in change efforts:

1. *Learn what constitutes a high-risk situation for relapse.* The more specific and detailed this inventory is, the more likely the client will recognize danger when it first appears. A high-risk situation for someone who has been chronically shy and withdrawn might involve being in the presence of identified aggressive, domineering people. One such client lists his immediate supervisor and father-in-law as the individuals who give him the most trouble. Furthermore, he is able to identify that he feels most intimidated when he is alone with these antagonists rather than in the company of others. Four days hence he is scheduled to have a monthly performance review with his boss, and that same evening he will be going to his in-laws' house for dinner.
2. *Identify the specific instances that are likely to arise in the future.* The client recognizes that when he encounters aggressive people, especially older men who remind him of his father, he reverts to withdrawn, passive behavior. Then he tells herself that all progress has been lost.
3. *Develop coping skills that will be needed to negotiate these obstacles.* The client is equipped with the means to avoid individuals who are considered high risk. Because in this case, this is not possible, he practices several well-rehearsed methods to help him come out of his shell and behave more assertively. He learns to confront aggressive individuals

through role-playing and participation in a group stocked with such personalities. Finally, he learns a half dozen ways to talk to himself in such situations so things don't get out of hand. Since it is highly likely that he will feel attacked sometime during the upcoming day with his boss and father-in-law, he has resolved that if he cannot manage to be assertive, he will at least avoid becoming withdrawn.

4. *Plan a lifestyle that alters the probability of temptations.* A toxic work situation filled with aggressive, insensitive peers was part of the problem this client faced. He acknowledged that it would be optimal to change his job. He also decided to no longer spend time with his older brother who continually berated and abused him verbally. He also recognized his option to avoid being alone in the company of his father-in-law. Once his confidence increased and he enjoyed success asserting himself in less risky circumstances, he could then "practice" with these more threatening targets.

Goal Construction and Attainment

There is nothing that dooms change efforts more than setting goals that are unrealistic or impossible to reach. Sometimes clients get so carried away in their enthusiasm that they aim for unreasonable objectives. Other times, ignorance leads them to go after changes that will unlikely be within their grasp.

In summarizing what is most likely to help people reach and maintain their objectives, Gollwitzer (1999) lists 12 factors to consider:

1. *Goal definition.* When goals are constructed in such a way that they are appropriately challenging, they are more likely to be reached and more easily maintained.

2. *Goal specificity effect.* General, vague goals, such as "I will try to work on this," don't work nearly as well as those that are specific: "I will make three phone calls to find out the information we discussed."

3. *Feedback and self-monitoring.* Goals tend to be maintained longer if the person receives consistent and accurate feedback on progress.

4. *Goal proximity effect.* Goals that can be worked on immediately are better than those that are planned for the distant future.

5. *Learning goals.* Rather than basing success on identified performance outcomes, it is preferable to devise learning goals that are more process-related. For instance, instead of saying that you will read the rest of this book by Wednesday, you could say that you will spend one hour reading each night before you go to sleep.

6. *Promotion goals.* One reason it is far more difficult to make changes last than to initiate the changes in the first place is that the former depends on avoiding negative outcomes (relapse) whereas the latter focuses on achieving positive objectives.

7. *Self-regulatory skills.* Maintaining change depends on a person's ability to remain goal-directed, avoid temptations, and recover from lapses before they become a more serious relapse.

8. *Conflicting goals.* There are always alternative paths available that directly conflict with intended outcomes. A person may be serious about curtailing drinking, but this desire may be at odds with expectations of friends at social gatherings. It is necessary to be well-prepared for dealing with these difficult choices.

9. *Creative integration.* Goals are more easily maintained when a person thinks of ways to make them part of his or her normal lifestyle. For example, a student who wishes to change poor habits related to studying may decide to hang out with others who spend their time studying together.

10. *Flexibility.* It is easier to avoid temptations and relapse if someone has multiple ways of getting his or her needs met.

11. *Preplanning.* Rehearsal and practice help prepare a person to deal with unforeseen obstacles and unanticipated challenges.

12. *Automatization.* This means making responses automatic and habitual so that conscious thought is unnecessary.

People have much less control over their behavior than they think. This is especially the case with habits that are often automatically elicited by stimuli in the environment (Bargh & Chartrand, 1999). Therapists must spend time helping clients develop habits and patterns that don't require a great degree of cognitive energy.

Practice

When a behavior is practiced to the point that it becomes automatic, there is increased probability that it will be maintained. When this practice takes place over a longer period of time, rather than concentrated within short intervals, the likelihood is even greater that success will continue. Furthermore, practice sessions are most effective when they resemble the actual situations in which the behavior is to be used. In addition, Lebow (1999) suggests that skill acquisition is maintained when practice is challenging enough to maintain interest and provides opportunities for feedback so that performance can be enhanced.

Structuring opportunities for practice for clients who wish to change specific behaviors is relatively simple. Far more challenging are those situations in which clients struggle with more existential issues related to finding meaning, assuming personal responsibility, or dealing with generalized anxiety. Even more difficult are clients who present the type of personality disorders or severe depression that transcends specific behavior change. In such cases, the goal involves transforming a more essential, core part of a person's being. While practice still involves completing therapeutic tasks, both in session and outside, the target behaviors tend to be geared toward successive approximation of ultimate goals.

A woman has been struggling with severe depression throughout most of her life. While antidepressant medication has been moderately helpful in controlling her mood disorder, she still engages in isolating behavior. During times when she actually needs contact the most, she may rarely interact with others. In the assortment of talk therapies she has already tried, she has developed a clear understanding of the biological basis for her depressed moods, as well as the psychogenic origins of her troubles. She consistently makes solid progress after seeking treatment (probably more the result of the medication), but after several months of stabilization, she experiences a relapse. She needs more practice in developing coping mechanisms to combat her withdrawal and isolation. Naturally, the ideal time for such practice is when she is feeling relatively good so that the strategies can be sufficiently habituated to rely on when she is not at her best.

Support Systems

In the case just described, or in any other for that matter, maintenance of change depends on the support available to encourage, reinforce, and sustain the efforts. Especially when the individual is isolated and feels alone, there are fewer resources available to draw upon when needed. Sometimes, "Thatta a girl!" is all that's needed; other times, far more help is required.

Based on their research with addicts who were able to maintain their recovery, Rogers and McMillin (1992) found that an effective support system:

1. Is available when the client needs it.
2. Includes multiple sources in case one doesn't work out or someone isn't available.
3. Is there for the person in spirit and friendship, but does not foster co-dependency by rescuing or baling the person out.

4. Provides honest, sensitive, and constructive feedback.
5. Offers good role models for the client to emulate.

A support system of helpers and advocates isn't worth much unless the individuals are readily available when they are needed. That is the reasoning behind "sponsorship" in 12-step programs—a sponsor makes himself or herself accessible at a moment's notice when there is a risk of relapse.

One of the reasons that changes people make during workshops, retreats, and while attending conferences often don't last, is because there is no ongoing support after the experience ends. It is easy to experiment with new behaviors, try out new strategies, or think about novel ideas while living in an enriched environment. But once people return to their usual lifestyle, they often lose the support and guidance that has encouraged them to take risks. Unless there is some generalization of what was learned, regression to previous patterns is highly likely.

Transfer of Learning

Changes are more likely to become permanent if behavior learned under one set of circumstances can be applied to other situations. Termed "spread of effect" or "generalization" by behaviorists, the principle is that lasting changes stem from a person's ability to respond flexibly to new challenges that arise (Sulzer-Azaroff & Mayer, 1991).

In contrast, change is *not* maintained when:

1. Reinforcements for current behavior are stopped or attention for good behavior ceases.
2. New behavior is punished.
3. Previous behaviors are reinforced
4. Stimuli prompt unwanted behavior.

Behavior tends to be maintained when a person is able to selectively attend to those stimuli that are most reinforcing and ignore those that are not. For instance, relationship-enhancing attributions occur when a person consistently perceives someone else's behavior as indicative of his or her finest traits and believes that any negative actions are the result of external factors beyond one's control (Holtzworth-Munroe & Jacobson, 1985). A similar process can take place when someone chooses to focus only on those factors that are most likely to support preferred changes.

In the case of religious or political conversion, as another example, faith is maintained in the face of irrefutable conflicting evidence by spending time with true believers who are likely to support the new beliefs. Contact is avoided with nonbelievers and those who might distract or sabotage progress, as in the structure of Alcoholics Anonymous and other self-help groups.

Baumeister (1994) believes that people can take an active role in maintaining their desired changes by structuring their personal contacts in specific ways. Avoiding situations and people who might challenge new loyalties is one way of enhancing conditions for enduring change.

Surviving Trauma

In their book on the transformational potential of trauma as a change stimulus, Tedeschi, Park, and Calhoun (1998) investigated a wide range of disasters, as well as their effects on survivors. While "traumatologists" usually focus on well-documented negative impacts such as prolonged grief, depression, decompensation, poverty, and posttraumatic stress, these researchers chose to examine the positive growth that can emerge from such experiences. Gathering together a group of researchers with similar interests, the authors thought to ask people who had been victims of crime, disaster, disability, illness, and social upheaval what they learned from the trauma and subsequent recovery.

That which doesn't kill you makes you stronger. According to Aldwin and Sutton (1998), surviving a traumatic experience can indeed, under certain circumstances, lead to a number of benefits, including:

1. Increased coping skills.
2. More flexible problem solving.
3. Increased pain and frustration thresholds.
4. Improved self-confidence.
5. Altered perspective and values.
6. Increased social support.
7. Higher self-esteem.

It is interesting how individuals who suffer the same misfortune can react so differently. Subjected to an earthquake, debilitating disease, kidnapping, car accident, or death in the family, some people fall apart and are never able to recover, while others show a degree of resilience that changes their lives for the better. The same can hold true for any number of other challenging circumstances that people manage to survive.

Whether a traumatic experience leads to growth or devastation depends on several factors, mainly the preexisting stress levels of the person, but also his or her personality and disposition. Some people have a tendency to make the best of things while others adopt a far more dysfunctional style of blaming things on external forces.

Whether involving a heart attack, infertility, cancer, childhood sexual abuse, loss of children or spouses in car accidents, or surviving a sinking ship, painful traumas were often cited as major platforms for instigating positive changes that persisted even a decade later when follow-up studies were done (Cohen, Hettler, & Pane, 1998). Sometimes these effects even grow over time. In one study of first-time heart attack victims, 12% reported that the experience produced constructive lifestyle and personal changes soon after the cardiac event. Remarkably, however, when they were checked 8 years later, that figure doubled: one quarter of the patients reported that the heart attack resulted in positive changes that had become a permanent part of their behavior (Affleck, Tenned, Croog, & Levine, 1987). Studies conducted two decades after sexual abuse and other traumatic experiences showed changes that remained relatively stable or grew in magnitude over time (McMillen, Zuravin, & Rideout, 1995). In one study of divorced women, conducted 10 years after the event, over 40% sustained long-term personal gains (Wallerstein, 1986). They developed new careers and became more self-sufficient and assertive. Of course, economic factors would also be a moderating variable for the 60% who didn't experience positive changes in their lives as a result of their single status.

Hardiness

While the posttraumatic growth researchers look at the types of individuals—their personalities, cognitive styles, and social situations—who are most likely to be transformed in positive ways, they do not often address enduring effects. Quite often when people suffer heart attacks or financial ruin, they vow to do things differently in the future, but within a few years (or even weeks) they find themselves in trouble once again.

It appears, however, that those who demonstrate hardiness (Florian, Mikulincer, & Taubman, 1995; Kobasa, 1979), psychobiological toughening (Dienstbier, 1992), or psychological resistance (Harvey, 1996; Rutter, 1987) seem to be the most resistant to relapses. They deal with stress. They metabolize setbacks by taking them in stride. They have vast internal resources for responding to unforeseen or unpredictable situations. They feel a sense of power over their lives, at least the part they can control. They are highly adaptable. Finally, they have what Meichenbaum (1985) calls "stress inoculation"—meaning they have developed progressive tolerance (through exposure and practice) to stressful events in such a way that they can cope more easily with setbacks.

Among the "trait" characteristics reviewed by Tedeschi, Park, and Calhoun (1998), it is the latter "state" condition that lends itself more readily to training. In other words, whereas "toughening" may be connected to physiological arousal (reduced endocrine responses to stress) and "hardiness" related to personality characteristics in which people are naturally optimistic and flexible, various cognitive strategies may also be learned in order to promote more enduring changes. A number of cognitive therapists (Beck & Freeman, 1990; Ellis, 1995; Ludgate, 1995; Meichenbaum, 1985) have developed specific procedures for stress inoculation, relapse prevention, and change maintenance. These are discussed in a later chapter.

Positive Expectations

Try a simple test. Using a scale of 1 to 10, 10 being "absolutely certain" and 1 being "pretty unlikely," rate the probability that you will maintain the changes you have begun. This test often predicts quite well the prognosis for lasting change. Unless there is a great expectation of success, the probability of relapse is quite high (Allsop & Saunders, 1989).

The therapist's role is often critical in helping clients refashion their expectations and feel increased hope for the future. A sense of hope is not only instrumental in accelerating changes in the first place, but also in keeping things going.

When clients leave their last session, even if they don't feel the greatest optimism for their continued recovery, they still put on their best face. After all, they don't want to disappoint their hardworking therapist who gives such an inspirational rah-rah speech to conclude their work together. On the other hand, if they were actually feeling doubtful that the effects of their treatment would last, then they probably would not be saying goodbye in the first place. It is, therefore, often difficult to get an honest reading of how clients are really doing with respect to their hopes for the future. That is one reason why follow-up sessions are so important after treatment has been completed.

Internal Dialogue

Whether a trauma leads to destructive or growth outcomes depends, in part, on how the victim chooses to view the circumstances. Depending on the theoretical orientation, this is called "the internal dialogue," "constructed meaning," or "cognitive structure." All of these processes result in a perception of events that allow the person to imagine that good things will happen.

Compare, for example, the ways different individuals talk to themselves internally about what they have experienced. Depending on how they choose to think about what matters—and it *is* a choice—they experience very different results:

"I'm a victim."	"I'm a survivor."
"I deserved this."	"I'm not exempt from facing adversity."
"God is punishing me."	"God is giving me a message."
"Why does this sort of thing always happen to me?"	"This only happens rarely, however frustrating."
"There is no hope."	"I can and will recover."
"There's no point in even trying."	"This is just a challenge to overcome."
"I have no options."	"There are some things I can control and others I can't."
"This is so senseless."	"There is a lesson to be learned from this."

Therapists can't deal with the irrational thinking without addressing the underlying belief structure (Beck, 1997). Relapse occurs when attention is directed only toward the symptomatic thought disorder but not the basic internal philosophy.

For example, a therapist can attack the surface cognitive statements—"It's terrible that the relationship didn't work out"—but unless he or she also looks at the more basic underlying belief, the client is unlikely to experience lasting change. In this case, the person is saying to herself deep down inside, "I don't deserve to be happy." Even experienced cognitive therapists are so delighted to identify irrational beliefs they immediately recognize that they make the mistake of looking no further.

In addressing the problem of maintaining changes initiated through cognitive therapy, Ellis and MacLaren (1998) recommend a number of therapeutic principles:

1. Remind clients that it is the nature of change efforts for behavior to improve at times, then to stop improving, and sometimes to slip backward. This is not only part of the natural process of evolution, but should be expected.
2. During times of *temporary* regression, remind clients to choose internal statements that worked previously.
3. Separate failures in behavior from labeling oneself a failure as a person. "Although it is preferable to succeed, when I don't do as well as I had hoped it is not the end of the world, nor does it mean that I am a failure."

4. Remember that it is a personal choice not to follow through on commitments. Long-term change requires hard work and practice; there is no easy substitute.
5. Don't delude yourself into thinking that you have ever arrived at a point at which you no longer have to be vigilant or work against the natural tendency to be lazy and inattentive.

Personal Meaning

Relapse is not an outcome but rather an ongoing process with a series of decision points along the way (Brownell et al, 1986). This means that intervention is possible anywhere along the backsliding path (Ludgate, 1995).

Lapses become relapses in the context of a client's experiences and how he or she chooses to interpret them. Once responsibility for outcomes is abandoned, the downward slide tends to accelerate.

There are several questions that therapists may ask to help with the process of assuming greater personal responsibility and creating more meaning in what is learned:

- What sense do you make of what happened?
- How does this fit into the context of your background and current situation?
- How has this been familiar to you?
- Which "narratives" or "old tapes" are used to account for this?
- To what or whom do you attribute influences and causes?
- What beliefs are operating internally?

Perceptual shifts, which are so crucial in maintaining altered beliefs over time, occur when a personal story is rewritten in such a way that it becomes part of one's permanent internal record (Baumeister, 1994). Narrative approaches to therapy help people become more involved as authors in the process of reconstructing their life stories (Monk, Winslade, Crocket, & Epston, 1997; White & Epston, 1990). This process can occur, such as in the case when relationships are beginning or dissolving. In the case of the former, couples are more likely to romanticize their first meeting as a stroke of wonderful luck, whereas during divorce proceedings they often see the same incident as the result of mutual convenience or an accident (Vaughan, 1986).

It is not sufficient, however, to help people rewrite their stories. These more healthy and constructive narratives must actually be "published," or put into print so to speak, so that commitments can be maintained over time.

Follow-Up

One final thought before we move on to clinical applications of these concepts: The natural deterioration effects that occur after most treatment can be minimized or prevented with scheduled follow-up sessions designed to monitor progress, make needed adjustments, and support efforts. Sometimes, maintenance treatment may be required for the remainder of a client's life, even if only once or twice a year, in order to ensure that changes persist.

From the outset, it is extremely important that therapists help clients create conditions in their lives that will lead not only to constructive and desired changes, but also to maintenance of those changes. Sometimes, what facilitates the initial surge of change momentum is different from what sustains it over time.

8
CHAPTER

Adjunctive Structures That Sustain Change

The therapeutic activity of promoting change is distinctly different from the task of maintaining its effects. Certainly care should be taken as part of the initial treatment to plan for relapses and maintenance of progress, but a distinctly different battle strategy is needed for defending one's position than for capturing new territory.

In his landmark manual of military strategy Hart (1954) reviewed battles spanning from the Greek-Persian War of 500 B.C. through World War II. In describing offensive campaigns in which the likes of Alexander, Caesar, Cromwell, Napoleon, Grant, and McArthur attempted to conquer enemies, or even when generals such as Lee were vastly outnumbered, a set of tactics favoring surprise, an indirect approach, and leverage was most successful. Yet in a defensive engagement in which the job is to protect hard-fought gains, a strategy of "elastic defense," which allows one to respond with a host of options from strategic withdrawal to counterattack, is preferred.

A different attitude and strategy are required to train troops for a long defensive siege rather than all-out offensive charge against an entrenched enemy. The same analogy holds true in the practice of medicine in which aggressive, invasive procedures are undertaken to treat acute problems, whereas the strategy for aftercare involves doing the least possible to maintain progress.

Similarly, in describing the dynamics of addiction treatment failure, Buelow and Buelow (1998) point out that the job of preventing relapse involves a different mindset and strategy than the original intervention. For one thing, maintenance must be viewed as a lifetime enterprise, one in which one must always be on guard for dangers, temptations, regression, and lapses.

Maintenance Tactics

In a previous chapter we examined the process by which a lapse can become something far more serious if left unchecked. The first question to be asked is whether it is a momentary mistake or misjudgment. Is the lapse observed by the client or does it go unnoticed? What does the person say to himself or herself about the event? Is it seen as significant or inconsequential? What sort of thinking follows the experience?

Compare, for example, these two sets of internal responses:

Hey, no big deal. Everyone slips up at times. Besides, I can handle this no problem. I don't think it even matters too much. It's not really a setback anyway because I could regain control any time I want. I just don't want to yet."

"Oh no! This is what I feared the most—that the changes wouldn't last. Gotta get control of myself. Can't let things get out of control. Just because I slipped up this one time doesn't mean I have to return to what I was doing before. This is only a test. And I can handle it because I've prepared for just this situation."

Lapses can be framed in an assortment of ways—as the beginning of deterioration or the first in a series of predictable challenges to be overcome. Certain attitudes like optimism or pessimism are significant in affecting this outcome. We know from treatment in general that placebo effects influence outcomes and that if people believe they will get better, they are much more likely to do so than if they are skeptical or feeling hopeless (Frank & Frank, 1991). It has even been estimated that as much of 15% of therapy outcomes are determined by the client's sense of hope (Lambert, 1992). The same holds true for maintaining progress in medical conditions (Weil, 1995) as well as psychological problems (Snyder, Michael, & Cheavens, 1999), as long as the placebo effect remains active.

Watch Yourself

Self-monitoring is absolutely critical to making changes last. This means continually asking yourself:

- "How am I doing?"
- "What sticky situations might I face next?"
- "How can I deal with what is coming up?"

People don't often listen to themselves or monitor very carefully what they are experiencing inside. In order to sustain change, it is imperative that the earliest signs of discontent or temptation are identified as early as possible. One can't, for example, do much to prevent a relapse if he or she doesn't realize there has been regression.

Keeping a record of activity also helps to remind the client what works best in which situations and what seems least helpful. This can be in the form of a journal, activity log, or more informal structure such as the following entry that was actually written on a long piece of toilet paper. The author is a woman who has had a series of destructive, exploitive relationships with men which, she has previously been unable to stop. She kept returning to the same men even though she was setting herself up for repeated disappointment. Just when she extricated herself from one loser, she seemed to immediately find another.

While at a party, she recognized a man she used to date across the room. She could feel a great number of negative feelings start to flood over her. Almost against her will she could feel herself being pulled toward him, even though he hadn't yet seen her. Inside her head she was telling herself all the right things she had practiced, but they weren't working. Recognizing this, she immediately retreated to a bathroom.

> "I'm sitting in here with a pen but with nothing to write on but the walls and toilet paper, so this will have to do. But must write smaller or this stuff will tear. I'm hiding here because I'm not ready yet to face what's waiting for me outside. Kevin is here, which I never expected, and I just know he's going to approach me and ask me to go home with him. I just don't trust myself even though I promised myself that those days were over."
>
> "I've got to get my shit together before I walk out of here. I wonder why the usual stuff isn't working? I've been practicing telling myself over and over, 'There I go again,' but it's not working. I know I'm about to make the same mistake, but I can't seem to help myself."
>
> "Okay. Time to make a plan ..."

This was a woman who was clearly committed to maintaining the changes she had initiated, even though she was not yet completely stabilized. Because she was aware of her vulnerability, she protected herself from acting out by retreating to a safe place in order to regain her composure and focus. She knew what was happening—she could actually feel the relapse evolving—because she was paying such close attention to what was going on inside her.

During the process of self-monitoring, it is helpful to complete the following steps:

1. *Anticipate dangers.* Just as a scout operating in enemy territory observes very carefully for the slightest sign of danger, so too must clients remain vigilant for traps and temptations.
2. *Identify triggers.* These are the traps that could spring with little warning. Because it is impossible to anticipate them all, a client may find himself or herself standing on top of a landmine, hearing only the tell-tale click that the mechanism has been activated.
3. *Notice warning signs.* There are signals inside, as well as in the outside world, that warn that vulnerability has been increased significantly.
4. *Review past mistakes.* The triggers, signals, and warning signs can best be anticipated if systematic study is undertaken of what has already gone awry.
5. *Monitor thinking.* Once in the midst of a lapse, it is important to check honestly and thoroughly what is going on inside one's head.
6. *Observe carefully.* Taking a step back can help one remain objective and detached from the situation. This can be done by viewing oneself as a neutral observer, or even a scientist, who is watching from behind a mirror.
7. *Graph progress.* This involves measuring the effects of interventions and choices, noticing what works best, and keeping a record of progress over time.

In his book on preventing relapses related to stress, Meichenbaum (1985) makes the point that while self-observation is a necessary strategy, it is not sufficient to counteract inertia. Becoming aware of what they are feeling often doesn't stop people from falling backwards. They might notice that they aren't really hungry, yet they still reach for the bowl of candy.

The second phase of maintaining change according to Meichenbaum is to help clients to talk to themselves internally, to initiate a dialogue not unlike the devil and angel sitting on the shoulders of the cartoon character. This conversation is actually a kind of quiet rehearsal for behavior in the outside world.

A woman was sitting by the phone, staring at it intently, willing it to come alive with all her will. She was pretending she had magical powers—The Great Melinda, or Kreskin, or even Merlin—the power to get others to do her bidding. In this case, she was hoping beyond reasonable limits that her boyfriend, or rather *ex*-boyfriend, would call her as he promised. It was 1 hour and 35 minutes past the time he said he would call (but who was counting?) and she was feeling very sad—no, more than sad—she was angry, frustrated, and despondent. She reached for the phone and started to push the buttons, as if her hand were acting all on its own. Just as she heard the first ring, she hung up. This is what she was thinking inside her head.

"Damn, that was a close call! I can't believe I'm so weak and spineless that I would give in to this jerk. Of course he wouldn't call. That's why I dumped the sonofabitch in the first place: I can't trust him."

"But I miss him so. And I *hate* being alone. Sometimes I think it's better to be stuck in a dead-end relationship with him than to come home to an empty house. And I miss him. Yeah, I know. I already said that."

"It's good that I miss him though. I can't just expect to end a relationship like this and then go about my life as if nothing happened. I loved the guy after all, even if he wasn't good for me."

"Well, maybe it wasn't as bad as I remember it was. We had some good times together. Even with all the yelling and games, sometimes ..."

"Oh, that's a lie! It wasn't good for a very long time. And if I pick up the phone right now and call him he'll be over in 5 minutes. That will feel good—for tonight, and maybe even tomorrow, but then the same crap will start happening all over again. I've been through this with him so many times."

"Okay, but I still want to talk to him. For just a minute. I just want to say hi. See how he's doing. Surely, there's no harm in that."

"I'm like an addict. It starts with a little nibble, a tiny, innocent, harmless gesture. Then before I can help myself, I'm hooked all over again. Got to do it cold turkey. Got to keep control over myself."

"So, who can I call instead? Or better yet, what can I do to occupy myself?"

Clients may believe this is a lot of work, but the whole dialogue takes place within a minute or two. With practice, it even becomes abbreviated into code phrases that act as reminders. We must remind clients, as well, that hard work is what maintaining change is all about.

Ringing Bells

The big question, though, is how someone is going to know when he or she is at risk for a setback. People must "hardwire" themselves so that they hear alarm bells ringing when they face threatening situations. This is not unlike what they have learned to do with any other set of behaviors. For instance, when I am leading therapy groups I have programmed myself to recognize the dozen or so instances when I must intervene. These might include when someone speaks for others, starts to ramble, or shows signs of acute distress. In these and other situations, I hear this little bell in my head that signals I must do something—right now! I may not know exactly what I should do, but I recognize that some decisive action is required or someone is likely to get hurt. Most people have learned to do something similar in the arenas in which they are most familiar at work and play.

Therapists often coach their clients in this area with an intervention along the following lines:

"It is time to program yourself with ringing bells whenever you face those situations that are most likely to sabotage your change efforts. For the lady hiding in the bathroom, this might be seeing an old flame. For others, it could be an old hang-out or a crisis event."

Clients would be wise to recognize the following early warning signs as part of their self-monitoring (Ludgate, 1995):

- Sleep disruptions
- Appetite changes
- Problems with memory or concentration
- Negative thinking such as brooding, guilt, shame, hopeless thoughts, disasterizing
- Increased anxiety
- Emotional outbursts
- Apathy and loss of energy
- Withdrawal or isolation

These symptoms are also indications of emotional problems other than relapse. Training clients to become better tuned to the rhythms of their bodies and minds can help them recognize immediately when such signs indicate that something isn't quite right. The challenge, of course, is not just for the client to discover when he or she is experiencing stress, but to recognize it early enough to intervene before a downward spiral begins.

Therapeutic Rituals

The use of therapeutic rituals often helps to sensitize clients to at-risk situations so they can reprogram responses that had previously been maladaptive. A ritual is a uniquely human symbolic act that organizes our lives. Greetings, bedtime stories, coffee breaks, family traditions, and ceremonies are all rituals. They spark a regimented series of steps that make following through on actions effortless.

When we ask someone what their favorite rituals are, they are likely to give us a blank look at first. But if we explain that they are the symbols that empower our memories and compel our commitment we may see a nod of recognition. As therapists, we use such rituals all the time. When we first greet clients at the door, we usually say the same basic things, "Won't you come in?" or "I'm ready to see you now" or "How have you been doing?" There are rituals associated with where each of us sits in the room, how we begin the conversation, and especially how we end it. There is a ritual about scheduling the next appointment and a 100 others that keep the process humming along.

We often help clients to construct therapeutic rituals as maintenance tools, teaching them to follow an orderly sequence of behaviors just as they do when they first wake up. Most people organize their lives in such a way that the first half hour upon waking is invariant. We tend to wake up at the same time, stretch with the same routines, and follow a prescribed order of urinating, brushing teeth, taking morning pills, showering, grooming, and dressing (always putting the same leg through jeans first). We usually eat the same foods for breakfast, read the paper in the same way, and manage to transport ourselves to work following the exact same route. We are creatures of habit because it is easier and requires little thought, freeing us up for far more important matters.

We would no sooner think about skipping our teeth-brushing ritual than we would forget to put on our right sock before our left one. Our brains have been grooved in such a way that these rituals maintain consistent behavior (Bargh & Chartrand, 1999). The same sort of thing must happen with any long-term change.

The challenge is to help clients create new rituals that they are prepared to maintain for the rest of their lives. Therapy actually represents a small portion of time in a person's life—just an hour a week for possibly a few months or so. Because we are not interested in keeping people dependent on us for the rest of their lives, we devise structures—rituals—that are designed to keep people going when we are not around.

"Every time you face a stressful situation like that in the future," we instruct a client with a history of panic disorder, "you are going to take a deep breath and slowly follow what you have learned. Then you are going to repeat to yourself the reminders about what is really going on . . ."

Another client with compulsive rituals is schooled in alternatives that are designed to break up the automatic, dysfunctional behavioral chains. "When you leave the house, instead of going back to check to see if you left the gas stove on—four different times—you are going to place your keys in the palm of your outstretched hand. Then . . ."

Metaphorical rituals are so much a part of therapeutic work. A client with prolonged grief reaction, who has been depressed and despondent for 3 years after her husband left, is invited to bring in a wedding picture. She is directed to say good-bye to her ex-husband (who is now remarried with a new baby), to recite reminders of all the ways her life has been enhanced since the marriage ended, and to burn the photo in the wastebasket. The ashes are collected and placed in a special urn where they are stored until the ritual is repeated, always on the first day of the month, until the past loses its hold over her.

A lonely, agitated client who can barely put together a complete sentence without breaking into tears, is invited to bring in his favorite childhood toy, an old, ratty teddy bear. He is directed to sit in a rocking chair with the stuffed bear on his lap and to draw strength and comfort from this sacred object that becomes like a totem. Not surprisingly, he finds his voice, which is articulate, clear, and without doubt. The man is ordered to keep the teddy in his backpack at all times during the next several months, out of view, but present nevertheless. He is told that he will feel its comfort and power just through this constant presence. Even now, 2 years later, the bear sits atop his computer screen as a reminder of the changes he has made.

The members of a men's group were struggling with their sense of personal identity. They felt lost and rudderless, not just in the way the group had been proceeding but also in their lives. The leader arranged for them to spend a long weekend in a wilderness area where they did some deeper work that involved building a sweat lodge together and revealing themselves around a ceremonial fire. The image was forever burned into their memories of the support they felt in the company of their peers while looking up at the stars and observing their skin sending up little vapor trails of steam. It became a turning point for the group and years later they could retrieve that image with perfect clarity.

Rituals of any form are created so that forward progress, like any other regular habit, will become automatic in the future. In an article about what sustains exercise programs throughout a person's lifetime, Keegan (2000) laments that the problem is rarely about people not knowing what to do. "We all know how to work out," he writes. "There are whole bookstores filled with advice, television programs, dozens of magazines, advice that all boils down to a few hard facts you already knew: Eat right, do aerobic workouts, and lift weights" (Keegan, 2000, p. 72). So, he asks, if people know what do, and know it is good for them, why don't they keep doing it? It is simple, he says: people are just not mentally tough enough. And they don't build in the kind of rituals that sustain them over time.

Just think about all the cross-country ski machines, stationary bicycles, rowing machines, weight benches, and other exercise equipment gathering dust in people's basements or serving as clothes hangers in people's bedrooms. They start out with the intention of doing vigorous exercise every week of their lives, but somewhere along the line they lose their will.

After interviewing exercise consultants and sports psychologists to world-class athletes, Keegan found that the key to their success was improving a person's resilience, flexibility, and commitment, especially when faced with stressful situations. This very point was illustrated by the earlier story of the man who recovered from a lapse in his exercise program. It is all a matter of strengthening willpower through the incremental building of sound habits. For instance, exercise consultants found that what works in maintaining a lifetime exercise program best is building daily rituals that become so habitual and ingrained that the person would never dream of abandoning them.

An individual might begin with the ritual of getting up at the same time every day to add structure to his or her life. Another healthy habit is to drink eight glasses of water a day. After that has been accomplished over a period of several weeks, another ritual might be added, perhaps a 20-minute workout twice per week. This process continues until one's life is filled with healthy rituals that have become ingrained.

Cognitive-Behavioral Chains

Among the first signs that progress is about to be compromised takes place inside a client's head. Before someone acts, or doesn't act, he or she first thinks about the situation, perceives things in a particular way, and interprets a predicament in such a way that faulty decisions are made. The "cognitive-behavioral chain," described by Nelson and Jackson (1989), involves plotting the sequence of thoughts that eventually leads to relapse. The process of identifying specific thought patterns and becoming more attuned to such internal conversations helps to sensitize clients to the vicious downward cycle that can lead to relapse.

A man struggled with depression that was considered psychogenic in origin and was often exacerbated by disappointments in his work and personal life. He attempted to medicate himself with excessive eating— junk food, ice cream, and fried foods that his physician warned were creating havoc in his body. He had tried a number of different diets, each of which worked for a period of time, but eventually he succumbed to temptation.

The therapist helped him develop a cognitive chain of his thought reactions to specific triggers that could result in a relapse (Table 1).

By following this chain of thinking, the client was able to trace the slow deterioration of his resolve and commitment. Such a process of demoralization is slow, progressive, and insidious. Becoming aware of the way he tends to think when he first starts losing control, provided

TABLE 1. Sample Cognitive Chain

Event	Interpretation
I receive a negative evaluation from my supervisor.	This crap always happens to me. She has got it in for me.
I talked to my co-workers for support.	They don't understand what is going on. They just humor me.
I meet a friend for drinks after work to get some sympathy.	He agrees with me that this isn't fair and that I keep getting treated like a jerk.
I can't sleep that night because I am so worried about my job. I eat some ice cream to help me relax. Then I feel guilty.	This all happened because of what these assholes at work are doing to me. I can't help it if they are determined to get rid of me. There is no sense in even trying anymore.
I show up to work late the next morning because I didn't rest at all.	My boss gives me the evil eye again. She definitely has it in for me. No matter what I do, she is going to make sure that I fail.
I get frustrated working on an assignment and mess it up.	It just all feels so hopeless. What is the sense of even trying anymore? And this stupid diet doesn't matter if I am about to be unemployed. Eating is about the only pleasure I have left.
I leave work early, feeling depressed and tired. On the way home I stop at the store to buy some potato chips, chocolate chip cookies, and a half gallon of chocolate fudge ice cream.	This is the only thing that will make me feel better. I have to help myself relax or I will lose control completely. I will just cheat a little this one time and then go back on my diet tomorrow.

this client with a blueprint of what to expect. He could then be drilled to recognize the earliest signs of a forthcoming relapse and intervene before it is too late.

Introducing a Self-Help Program

Self-help recovery programs aren't far wrong when they insist, "once an addict, always an addict." We are all on the verge of relapse—of falling back into the abyss from which we once escaped, or more likely, crawled out many times.

In order for any of us to deliver on our promise to make a difference for our clients, they are going to have to give up their illusions. "Aha," they begin thinking immediately. "So that's the gimmick. *I'm* the one who's got to do all the work."

They are going to have to face the realities of what is involved in lasting change and the truth about a variety of illusions they preferred to ignore.

1. *"This is going to be easy."* This is the biggest lie of all. There is nothing harder, and they know it. Maintaining changes is a continual battle that must be fought every day. In some ways, it gets easier over time, but it can become more challenging when hard-won victories are taken for granted.
2. *"This is a great plan."* A self-help program simply provides a structure for organizing one's efforts. It typically simplifies matters dangerously, but with the benefit of giving someone a few simple rules to remember and follow. Such a program usually works only as long as an individual is prepared to abide by its guidelines. One example mentioned earlier is that one can lose weight successfully eating Jell-O, steak, or tofu, but the effects surely won't last unless he or she is prepared to continue this habit forever.
3. *"Once I'm in the clear, I can coast."* The effort never ends. We don't just initiate change, pat ourselves on the back, and then go on with the rest of our lives.
4. *"I'll get lots of help."* It is disconcerting for clients to discover that many of the same people who said they wanted them to change end up being the ones who try to sabotage their efforts.
5. *"This will make all the difference."* When this illusion is challenged, clients feel very discouraged. Many people have a misguided belief that once they make their long-fantasized change, their whole life will be turned around. It is downright depressing to discover they may still be unhappy and dissatisfied even though they are now skinny, married, employed, drug free, or following an exercise regimen. It's enough to make someone give up.

A therapist might explain the need to give up illusions in the following way:

"This is a heck of a way to begin our relationship together, by attacking your illusions. In order for me to deliver what I have promised, you are going to have to do your part as well. That begins with being honest with yourself about the amount of energy and commitment that is required in order to make desired changes last. If you truly want this to work, you will have to do some hard thinking about how much effort you are prepared to devote to this lifelong project. I promise to make the journey a bit easier by providing a structure to help focus your attention and maintain your momentum. Ultimately, however, *you* will be the one who decides whether you are done with falling backwards, tired of reading self-help books, bored with hearing yourself talk about the same old struggles, and frustrated with covering the same old ground over and over. It is time to begin anew. Take my hand and we will walk together."

Correcting illusions and recasting more realistic expectations are important initial steps for other changes that must follow.

Lifestyle Changes

The issues clients bring to us in therapy represent a relatively small part of their lives. They talk to us primarily about problems, things gone wrong, and people who annoy and disturb them. When they do let us in on other facets of their lives, they are selective about what they choose to reveal. With such limited data at our disposal, it's always hard for us to help clients integrate new gains into their lives.

Regardless of why clients initially consulted us, we may also address lifestyle changes that we believe are good for almost everyone. These might relate to a therapist's personal beliefs about the universal need for regular exercise, 8 hours of sleep per night, low-fat foods, or an extended group of friends. Hopefully these beliefs are based on research, rather than a desire to create clones of our own values.

Our job at this stage is essentially to help clients make lifestyle changes that support continued progress. Generally speaking, if a client is performing at optimal levels in all areas of personal functioning, then following through on aftercare tasks is going to be a lot easier.

Some of the lifestyle areas we might attempt to restructure include:

- spending habits
- friendships
- work
- social life
- recreational pursuits
- sleep schedules
- eating and exercise habits
- cultural identity
- spiritual and religious involvement
- education
- love life
- support groups

In each area, our job is to do whatever we can to help clients stabilize their lives and reorient their priorities so that changes might be more easily maintained. This is much more easily accomplished when clients have additional support along the way.

Working With a Partner

Since we can't be available to clients whenever they need us, it is extremely important to help them reach out to others who might be a good source of support. Such support is especially helpful after treatment formally ends.

One of the most useful aspects for clients of participating in therapy is learning a problem-solving method while focusing on presenting complaints. As they work through their own struggles, they are also introduced to a process that can be applied in many other life situations, without requiring the help of a professional.

An important therapeutic adjunct involves encouraging clients to recruit other helpers who can be "trained" to offer support as needed. This process applied to sustaining client change is also useful for therapists in various forms of peer supervision (Kottler & Hazler, 1997). The following steps would be helpful:

1. *Find someone you can trust.* Select one or more individuals in your life who would be willing and available to help as needed.
2. *Teach your partner how to help you.* Explain what you need and don't need from them. You don't want advice. You want someone who will listen and can be a sounding board.
3. *Describe the ways you feel stuck to your helper.* Stay away from talking about others and concentrate on talking about your own frustration and feelings that are elicited.
4. *Ask your partner to summarize the main themes heard so far.* You fill in with what is missed.
5. *List what you have already tried that has not worked.* The more exhaustive the inventory, the better a handle you can get on past mistakes and failures.
6. *Make a commitment to not do those things anymore.* This is a critical step in the process, one in which the client may demonstrate resistance. Even though past coping strategies may not be effective, they are still familiar and comfortable.
7. *Brainstorm a list of other options.* As with any such exercise, it is preferable to develop as many alternatives as possible. People often report feeling empowered just by the realization that there are many other options available to try.
8. *Try out some of the strategies generated.* Afterwards, provide feedback to your helper about what worked best.

Of course, we need to caution our clients not to replace therapy by professionals with such support from individuals who are neither prepared nor trained to assume the burden. A program such as this should simply become an adjunct to regular treatment.

☐ Transformative Travel as an Adjunctive Strategy

I'd like to cover one other therapeutic strategy in considerable detail because I think it is an untapped resource that has been largely ignored in the literature. I've often wondered if I might do more good as a travel agent than a therapist, especially when it comes to promoting lasting changes. It seems to me that many people have been more dramatically and irrevocably impacted by certain kinds of travel experiences than by personal therapy or supervision.

In this context, I am not referring to typical vacations or holiday retreats, but rather the kind of trip one takes in which he or she come back a completely different person. Furthermore, I have noticed that in a number of ways, the effects can last a very long time.

Background

For the past several years, I have been interviewing people who experienced therapeutic transformations as a result of their travels (Kottler, 1997; Kottler, 2000a; Kottler, 2000b). I have been particularly interested in what it was about their trips that produced life-altering experiences and if the change processes involved resemble what occurs in therapy.

Scant literature exists on this subject, with the exception of many interesting travel memoirs that document the kinds of personal changes that are possible (Persig, 1974; Lapierre, 1985; Abbey, 1990; Fraser, 1991; Thayer, 1993; Zurick, 1995; Krakauer, 1997; Bryson, 1998; Heat-Moon, 1999; Iyer, 2000) and novels that vividly depict the sorts of transformations that people undergo while immersed in different cultures (Tyler, 1985; Kingsolver, 1999).

While some attention has been paid to the ways that adventure-based activities can be used as adjuncts to therapy (Asher, Huffaker, & McNally, 1994; Gillis & Simpson, 1991), few attempts have been made to integrate structured travel as a part of what therapists do. This is particularly unfortunate considering the opportunities travel affords pilgrims to initiate changes that would be far more difficult on home territory.

There might, in fact, be a number of similarities between what happens in good therapy and what occurs in travel experiences that produce transformative, permanent changes. The idea behind this type of adjunctive therapeutic activity is that it provides ways for clients to practice what they are learning in sessions, stimulates new insights, and provides a structure for experimenting with new, more effective behaviors. As discussed earlier, this type of structure is crucial in order for changes to persist.

Change Processes in Travel

Many of the universal variables present in most forms of therapy are also found in transformative travel:

Mindset ripe for change. The placebo effect and the impact of constructive expectations can operate powerfully in transformative trips. Clients must be programmed to look for changes, to remain open to them, and to make themselves as accessible as possible to novel experiences that are so often associated with therapeutic gains.

Insulation from usual influences. One of the things that traveling can do that therapy cannot, is isolate clients from friends, family, and others who often control their lives. Time and time again, I have heard people say that they were able to reinvent themselves while on the road because nobody knew who they were, or who they were supposed to be. They could be anyone they wanted and nobody knew that was not the "real" them. The hard part, of course, is maintaining those changes upon return.

Getting lost. This is a very interesting metaphor, not only for travel, but for therapy. The best things seem to happen when we leave the planned agenda, throw away the map, and embrace whatever we encounter along the way. If everything goes as planned, at least in travel, the trip probably won't be remembered for very long afterwards. If we listen hard to the best travel stories, we often hear themes of facing adversity, challenges, discomfort, and fear. The real travel starts when people lose their way.

Emotional arousal. The emotional activation that takes place may explain why the most transformative travels are often extremely uncomfortable experiences. There is nothing like fear, anger, or anxiety to help us remember things for the rest of our lives. This emotional arousal can be transcendently positive as well—watching a sunset on a beach, sharing intimate moments with a loved one, or giggling in ecstasy.

Altered states and heightened senses. Our senses are at optimal functioning when we travel to a different environment. We smell, see, hear, and feel things that we would otherwise ignore back home.

We become far more sensitive to everything going on around us, and inside us. We are (over)stimulated by the novel stimuli. We become open to experiences that we would not otherwise attend to, or respond to, back home. In the language of hypnotic induction, we become far more susceptible to influence because we are in a more vulnerable state.

Movement through time, space, and place. There is something about being on the move, which travel represents, that makes us more open to new experiences. Routines and daily patterns are altered, making it easier to experiment with alternative ways of functioning.

Teachable moments. Nothing one learns on a trip cannot be learned back home; it is just easier to gain a different perspective when we are in the kind of receptive mood that accompanies travel.

Facing fears. Transformative travel is often about solving problems in new ways and facing what we fear the most. Especially in foreign cultures and very novel environments, we can't get our needs met in the usual ways. Misunderstandings and miscommunications are common. What we usually do does not work. In order to survive, we must invent or discover new ways to express ourselves, ask for help, and get needs met. If this lesson is generalized to the home environment, the traveler learns to be more flexible, resourceful, and proactive.

Time structured to promote novel experiences. One difference between a trip and our normal life is that we have the time to try new things, experiment with new ways of being and interacting, as well as to reflect on these experiences. Therapy often encourages people to do things that are good for them that they don't necessarily want to do. Travel often makes this not only possible, but imperative. If we want to find food or get from one place to another, we must do many things that are uncomfortable. The path of the pilgrim often involves suffering.

Public commitments of intentions. Now we get to the tough part—how to make changes last. Just as in group therapy, it helps if clients can be encouraged to make public commitments of what they intend to do differently in the future and how they are going to apply what they learned.

Process experiences systematically. This is where therapists come back into the picture. The impact of an amazing travel adventure or transformative experience can only be sustained if efforts are made to make sense of the experience, create personal meaning, and generalize from one situation to others. Keeping a journal during the travels often help in these areas. Our job is ask the difficult questions: "So what?" and "What now?" Such questions may take the following form:

"Okay, so you have had a memorable trip. You have learned a lot and had a magnificent time. You are positively glowing from the encounter. You say that this changed your life. Now prove it! Let's see what we can do together to apply what you learned to the many areas of your life that have characteristically given you trouble."

A Homework Assignment

Throughout my career I have appreciated feeling like a hypocrite when I didn't apply to my own life what I taught to my clients and students. This applies to the use of travel as an adjunct to therapy: In order to sell this method to others we must first to be able to apply it in our own lives. If we want our clients to be fearless risk takers, open to new experiences, resourceful, courageous, and self-sufficient, then we must lead where they can follow. We must be able to model in our own lives what we ask of them.

It is not necessary to travel to a foreign country, or even a different city, in order to experience therapeutic travel; it is just easier to make changes when we immerse ourselves in a different environment. In my work as a therapist, I have been frustrated by the limits of what can be done in face-to-face conversations that lack structured opportunities to practice what has been learned. Therapeutic adjuncts are valuable because they place such heavy emphasis on self-help resources that can be applied outside of sessions.

Travel is another valuable structure that not only provides homework opportunities for clients, but also supplies a metaphor for the therapy process as a whole. After all, therapists act as guides who lead people on journeys and, in the process, help them find their own way.

As with people who attend retreats, workshops, or any other intensive growth experience, clients face the difficult challenge of making the effects last after they return from a travel experience. So often, whatever people claim was so important gets lost in the daily grind of reentry to normal life. Our role as therapists is, therefore, critical to helping clients prepare for inevitable relapses and continue their forward momentum long after therapy ends.

The Certainty of Failure and Uncertainty of Change

We are approaching the end of our own journey together; the time when our collaboration must end. As an author, my job has been to try to influence you in ways not unlike the work we do as therapists. If you've gotten this far in the book, hopefully something you've read has changed you in some modest way. But like you, I have rather high expectations for my work. Why waste our time promoting changes if they aren't going to last?

This final chapter examines some of the realities of being a therapist and the need to accept the limits of what we can do. We must take our victories where we can get them, deal with the times when things don't go as well as we had hoped, and learn from our failures.

It Is Often the Little Things

It is very difficult to engineer lasting changes when we can't be certain which strategies matter the most. At times, the littlest, and often unintentional, things seem to have the greatest impact while at other times the most well-planned interventions appear to have no effect whatsoever.

Like most therapists, I have my theories about what I think makes the most difference in people's lives, especially when it comes to making changes last. At the same time, it is also humbling to confront how little we really know and understand about this phenomenon. Two examples of people reporting on something I have done that changed their lives stand out. In both cases, I offered about a minute of assistance without much conscious thought or effort. In contrast are those times when I have spent years with certain clients, week after week, doing everything in my power to offer help and never quite certain whether anything I did or said had any impact at all.

Every year I see a friend at a conference who never fails to remind me that I changed his life one day. We had been working together doing a workshop. In the middle of our presentation, I noticed that his digital watch was set not to the current time, but according to the time zone in which he lived. When I asked him why he didn't reset his watch, he shrugged helplessly.

"Want me to reset if for you?" I offered.

He backed away as if I intended to assault him. "Are you kidding?" he asked me. "Then I'd have the wrong time when I get back home."

"Not if I showed you to do it yourself," I pointed out.

He seemed grateful for my gesture but had such aversion to anything technological that he was very reluctant to get into this area. It seemed a lot easier just to make mental translations in his head.

"Are you sure?" I reached for his wrist but he pulled away abruptly. Still, I wasn't willing to give up. There are not that many things that I can do mechanically, but this happened to be one of them.

"I bet I could show you in two minutes," I challenged him.

"Okay," he said with a sigh, as if he was really just humoring me and had no intention of really learning this skill.

I went through the steps while he watched me. Then I asked him to do it while I corrected his technique. He broke out into a huge grin, just like a child riding his bike without training wheels for the first time.

Through the rest of the weekend, I continued to test him, just to make sure the learning stuck. It did.

What is the meaning of this tiny, insignificant interaction? Did this new-found watch adjustment competence translate into other areas of his life? I don't know for sure, but soon thereafter I received my first e-mail message from him. He had finally become Internet-savvy even though he swore he would avoid it like the plague.

The second case involved a new colleague who began her job on campus at the same time I had. We were both disoriented much of these first weeks, and I noticed that she was just as directionally challenged as I was. Yet she expressed great admiration for my navigational skills in getting us back to our building after we wandered somewhere for lunch.

"How do you do that so easily?" she asked me with genuine amazement. "You have been here only a few days just like me, but somehow you always find our building. I walked around lost for half an hour the other day."

"It's really quite easy," I told her. "You see that bell tower on the top of the building?" I pointed out this landmark.

"Yes?"

"Well, wherever you are on campus, you can always see it sticking out high above everything else. You just head right for it."

Of course this now seemed rather obvious to her, like many things that are often right before our eyes, but she had never noticed it before it was pointed out. From that day forward, she never got lost again.

This story would end there except this woman now greets me every time I see her by reminding me, and anyone else around, that I helped her to find her way when she was lost. This has made all the difference to her in her job and adjustment to her new life. Furthermore, ever since then, she looks for "bell towers" and other landmarks wherever she travels and no longer feels lost most of the time.

These two little incidents appear to have had lasting impact on others even though the effort expended was minimal. I could tell you many other stories in which I worked myself to misery trying every intervention I could think of, thinking constantly about the cases, consulting several different colleagues for supervision, reading everything I could get my hands on, all with little noticeable effect on the clients.

We prefer to think that our planned, intentional therapeutic interventions result in the swiftest, most enduring changes, but this is not always the case. While this phenomenon is certainly a continual source of delight and disappointment, it is also quite humbling to realize that with all our theories, research, and training, quite often we don't have a clue as to why some clients maintain their changes and others end up far worse than when we first met them.

☐ When Failures Are Instructive and Relapses Are Constructive

Failures and regressions can be valuable tools for learning. In some cases, they can be the most significant impetus for permanent change (Kottler & Blau, 1989; Kottler, 1999). In the short run, however, it may appear that all previous progress has been negated and the client is back to square one.

In our work as therapists, for instance, we may spend a disproportionate amount of time thinking and talking about cases in which things are not proceeding according to plan because clients seem resistant or appear to be even worse off than before they began treatment. Yet it is the nature of change that chaos and disorganization often occur during times of transition. Unfortunately, therapists often misinterpret such confusion, ambivalence, apparent inactivity, and inarticulation as signs of treatment failure rather than evidence of a period of gestation in which serious work is going on internally (Hager, 1992).

When people are asked about the critical incidents that most influenced their ongoing decisions to maintain difficult changes, they often talk about what they learned from their failures and relapses. In reality, failures teach us quite a number of things about our work and provide our clients with many valuable lessons.

Failure Promotes Reflection

Therapists focus more on the cases that are not going well than the ones that are following the planned agenda. We are haunted most by the clients we could not assist rather than those we did help. We invest more time and energy with clients who are struggling than with those who are doing well. Failures and disappointments force us to look more closely at what we are doing (and not doing), to consider other courses of action, and to find the sources of power and influence.

Our clients, as well, become obsessed with what is not working in their lives. They reconsider every part of their existence. They make new decisions about the future. They assess priorities and reassess basic values. Late at night and during odd moments, they think about where they have been and where they are going. In fact, they are in therapy in the first place because they have failed to help themselves. They are undertaking this journey of growth specifically as a result of some debilitating failure that got their attention.

With change, as well, it takes something dramatic to get people's attention and to force them to give up what is not working and try something else. Without failure and relapse, people would go on about their lives without stopping to consider where they are headed and why. Failures can thus be reframed as opportunities for further growth. This is the case not only with our clients, but also in our own lives.

Failure Stimulates Change

People become intensely motivated to discover some alternative strategy when their current one is no longer working. They may be in a miserable state of anxiety, fear, and depression, and may be immobilized by disorientation and confusion. It is our job to help them sort things out. We teach clients to face their fears and to use these crisis points as a staging area for growth and transformation.

I am writing these words at the beginning of my teaching/research assignment in Iceland. During my first month here I was perfectly miserable—lonely, depressed, disoriented, anxious, and literally so physically ill with the flu that I could barely get out of bed. It was dark all the time. I couldn't understand the language or the customs. I had no idea if my students were learning anything. I thought about nothing but going home. Only 135 days left . . .

If I had known what I would have faced, I would have never chosen to come here in the first place. Like my clients, I don't go looking for trouble; it just finds us during times of vulnerability.

As I took inventory after surviving the first month ("failure promotes reflection"), I reviewed my daily journal entries and noticed that I was not the same person I had been when I first arrived. I had learned to confront my loneliness, structure my time, adapt to a very foreign culture, and change my teaching strategies to fit a different student population. Living in chaos and excruciating discomfort each day forced me to make changes in the way I conducted my daily business. I learned a thousand new things about myself, the way the world works, and how to get my needs met. I learned to relax and let go.

In this third month, I have never been happier. My days are so filled with excitement and stimulation that I can barely sleep during the progressively shorter nights because I am so eager to get outside and start the next day. All of this happened, of course, because initially I took the risk to come here and immerse myself in another culture for half a year. Just as important is that because I was initially miserable and regressed to a level of basic functioning that could be generously called treading water, I was extremely motivated to do some things differently. The key factor, however, will be how much of these changes persist after I return home.

Failure Provides Feedback

Another way to define failure or relapse is simply as a source of feedback. "What was tried did not work," is what the outcome is saying. It is time to consider what happened ("failure promotes reflection"), make adjustments in what we are doing ("failure stimulates change"), and learn from the data available.

A therapist, for example, may decide to confront a client about a pattern of getting drunk on occasion, going to bars, picking up men who abuse her, and then becoming filled with guilt and remorse. He or she may sensitively suggest that continuously engaging in this destructive behavior might be based on a need to punish herself for being a lousy mother. The therapist may view this interpretation as brilliantly accurate and expertly framed because it was presented in a soft, gentle manner, using eloquent language, and with an effective style.

Unfortunately, instead of producing the desired moment of revelation, the therapist sees pure horror on the woman's face. She shakes her head in denial, says angrily that she has been misunderstood, and shows by her body language that she has withdrawn. The therapist, of course, interprets and confronts this behavior as well, telling her that running away from things isn't going to make them better. "After all," the therapist confronts her again, "isn't what you are doing right now *exactly* what you tend to do with others in your life? Isn't this what you wanted to change?"

The therapist is proud of using immediacy to bring the original confrontation from the past to the present and actually connecting her presenting problem to her current behavior. She might deny what she does with her drinking, but there is no way that she can avoid admitting how she is pouting in this moment. She has even reported before that this is how she gets herself into trouble in relationships. I've got her now, the therapist thinks.

Tears start to stream down her face and she begins to sob. Without saying a word, she gathers her things together and walks out of the office. She never looks back, keeps another appointment, or returns your calls.

So, what happened? Another resistant client who couldn't take the heat? Another case of a client so well-defended and in such denial that she wasn't ready to change? These explanations are a few of the many possibilities. Perhaps, the therapist thinks optimistically, she was cured by this brilliant confrontation and didn't need to come back. A more likely conclusion is that these interventions failed because they were deeper than the client could handle at that time. She shut down because she felt attacked rather than understood. She fled because she wasn't getting what she thought she needed most.

There is no way to find out what really happened with this woman (Believe me I tried because she was my client, and this is just what happened in our session.) As much as I would like to think that my therapeutic strategy was sound and my execution was flawless, I failed this client. I failed her not because I made a mistake or miscalculation, or even because I compounded this error by pushing her even harder. I failed her because I did not pay attention to the information she was giving me so clearly. She was saying, "No thank you. I don't want what you are selling right now."

I then responded to her by saying, "I know what is really best for you. Just hold still. Let me try it again. I am sure you will like this better now."

Again, she said no—this was not what she could hear in that moment and I ignored this valuable feedback. I did not learn from the information that she provided me. If I had, I am convinced I would have altered my strategy, backed off with the confrontation business, and just stayed where she was until she was ready to move further.

This case became a turning point for me as it led to some relatively permanent changes in my therapeutic style. I have long struggled with impatience, needing clients to get better according to *my* schedule rather than their own. Each time I catch myself pushing clients and students too hard, I see this woman's face. I see her hunched over in my chair, tears streaming down her face. I see her walking out and never coming back.

That is not to say that I am not vigorously confrontive in my work (and writing) because I am. Immediacy is still my favorite technique for building relationships and creating magical moments in sessions. I have learned, however, how to pay closer attention to what my mistakes, miscalculations, and lapses can teach me. I might do something stupid, even repeat it a second time, but I usually get it by the third time, which is plenty of time to recover.

Failure Encourages Flexibility

Relapses are good, I tell my clients. A little failure is just what you need, I tell my students. Most of the time, I believe this, but almost never when I am actually in the throes of disappointment.

It is when we confront our limits and face obstacles that can't be overcome using our usual strategies that we have to invent something quite new. Creativity finds it source in such failures.

For many years a therapist I know approached his work from the same theoretical perspective. He was an avid cognitive-behavioral therapist, and an exceptionally skilled one at that. He learned his methods well, memorized the core irrational beliefs, developed a dozen powerful teaching metaphors, and had his routines down so well that it resembled therapy by numbers. "You got some residual guilt mixed with lingering depression over childhood abuse? No problem. Try number 8."

Well, maybe I am exaggerating a little. Anyway, he was known far and wide for his effectiveness in treating various compulsive disorders, depression, and a host of other problems with cognitive distortions at their root. He was an expert in helping people quickly identify what they were telling themselves that was getting in the way and what they could substitute instead.

One day, while this therapist was on auto-pilot, challenging a client to give up his insane desire to be perfect in every aspect of his life, the man turned to him and told him that he was an asshole and that if he didn't back off, he might get punched in the face.

The therapist stopped in genuine surprise. He had been right in the middle of one of his favorite stories (told 100 times before, so he knew it always worked) when he was interrupted.

"Listen," his client told him. "I don't like what you are doing. You aren't even listening to me. You just like to tell your stories. I am sure that they are very good, and maybe other people get something out of them, but you aren't hearing what I am saying."

The therapist was dumbfounded by this scolding but didn't say a word in response, because he knew the client was right. He just nodded his head.

"So, what I would like to do," the client continued, "is NOT talk about this perfectionistic stuff, because frankly I happen to like this about me. For someone in my line of work, you have to be perfect. So, please stop trying to change that part of me and just listen for a moment. Okay?"

Rarely would a client ever be this direct and helpful in providing valuable feedback. Often, we must infer such messages from other cues (which I failed to do with the client who walked out on me). Nevertheless, this cognitive therapist was now prohibited from using his favorite methods. He had to abandon, virtually completely, a cognitive approach and resort to other styles that were long-buried in his past.

What this therapist learned from this encounter, which lasts until this day, is that he had to develop greater flexibility in his work. He was becoming burned out precisely because he had gotten so skilled and effective with one method. It is somewhat like the old saying that if all you have is a hammer, you look only for nails.

Although I used the example of a cognitive therapist, I have seen this pattern enough times with clinicians of many different theoretical persuasions. We all become comfortable with our favorite methods. We get into a groove in which we tell basically the same stories, use similar anecdotes, and approach cases the same way. This not only makes our work easier, but it is critical to applying interventions consistently and reliably. After all, who would like a surgeon to try doing a procedure a different way each time just to break up the monotony?

All things being equal, a therapist with lots of treatment options is more effective than one who relies on fewer approaches. It is preferable to have several methods available to reach an outcome so that if the first one does not work well, the therapist can move on to the next one, and the next one. As with our clients, we often don't abandon a favorite strategy in lieu of a less familiar one without a certain amount of kicking and screaming. We may need to face a brick wall, with no way to scale it or go around it, before we put aside our usual bag of tricks in order to discover something quite new.

Failure Improves Frustration Tolerance

According to Meichenbaum (1985) and others, the best way to prevent permanent relapses is to inoculate clients against them. This involves deliberately provoking setbacks so the person can become skilled in dealing with them. Skiing instructors, for example, teach beginners first how to recover from a fall, then push them down to dislodge their bindings so that they must practice putting them back on. It is important for beginners to do this over and over, until it becomes second nature. Then when (not if) they take a spill in an awkward area, rather than panicking, they know exactly what to do.

Failures and setbacks teach people to take disappointments in stride. As cognitive therapists are quick to remind us, the ways we react to situations strongly depend on how we choose to interpret them. I was supervising two co-therapists who were reacting very differently to the group they were leading together. The first one reported that the group members were ornery, hostile, and unmotivated and that nothing they tried had worked very well yet.

I asked the second leader if that was her take on things. "Well, kind of," she said, tilting her head as if she wasn't sure that was true. I could tell she was being loyal to her partner and didn't want to contradict her.

When I prodded her further, she gave a very different version of the proceedings. She didn't expect very much from the members in a first session anyway, so she was not particularly disappointed by their behavior. In fact, she found it perfectly reasonable that they would be cautious and hesitant (her preferred words instead of resistant and hostile). Sure, they had tried a number of interventions, none of which had gone over particularly well. But what she learned from the experience was just to remain cool, not get unduly frustrated, and be patient long enough for the members to feel comfortable.

What an awesome woman, I thought, as I looked over to her partner to see if she had been listening. Unfortunately, she was actually trying to contradict this version of the story and continue with the complaining, which I quickly cut off. I could see her becoming frustrated by this—the failure she had experienced in the group session was now repeating itself in the supervision meeting. She felt judged by me, and left wanting. She felt like a failure and decided she didn't like group therapy at all.

All of this came out a bit later and led to a marvelous discussion among the three of us. The lesson I reinforced, and one that I am emphasizing here, is that when things don't go the way therapists hope or expect, they can use it as an opportunity to work on their own tolerance for ambiguity, frustration, and disappointment.

Failure Teaches Humility

There is nothing like arrogance to get in the way of effective change efforts. Once we become overconfident and convinced that we can handle anything that comes up, then we put ourselves in a very vulnerable position. Because, sure enough, something or someone will come along to prove us wrong.

It always amazes me when I meet other therapists who act as though they know exactly what is going on with every case all of the time. They almost never appear confused or uncertain; furthermore, when I check out my perception, they shrug with a nonchalance that suggests that they really do feel that sure of themselves inside. I contrast this with the way I feel most of the time, and it drives me crazy.

My own instructors and supervisors constantly told stories about their miracle cures, describing incredibly complex cases in which they knew just want to do. Textbooks are loaded with case examples that prove the theories presented work just as promised. Workshop presenters show demonstration videos in which they promote virtually instant results from applying the methods they are selling. Group supervision sessions are often filled with participants who posture and present cases that make them look good.

What I have learned most from being a therapist is how tenuous, uncertain, complex, and confusing people really are. I have learned to live with my own "not knowing" about what is going on most of the time. I have managed to tolerate (although not nearly as well as I would prefer) the difficult situation of sitting with a person who desperately wants to know what is going on and only being able to offer tentative guidance.

I have great admiration and sympathy for the new briefer therapies that diagnose problems during the first session, and fix them during the next one to four sessions. I have even had great success with these methods, although if someone pressed me about how change really took place, I would have to plead ignorance. Like most therapists, I have my theories and guesses, some of which I like quite a lot. But doing therapy, and especially failing as a therapist, has taught me a lot about my own limits.

When changes don't last—and after all, nothing lasts forever—we are forced to take stock of where we have been, and where we are going next. I may curse my clients and students (at the time) for not cooperating with my plans. Why must they be so difficult, I mutter to myself? Why must this be such hard work?

In the end, I am left in wonderment. What I love most about this work is that I will never truly understand what change is all about, much less what makes it last. I can spend a whole other lifetime in this field and still not come close to the mystery of what leads people to transform themselves for as long as they remain alive. I do think, however, that we are getting closer and closer to the mark, that is, if we have the courage to admit what we don't know or understand.

EPILOGUE

I went to the dentist a few days ago for my semi-annual teeth cleaning and checkup. There was a fresh-faced, newly minted hygienist assigned to my case. I could tell she was a recent graduate because of all the equipment she was wearing—not only the usual rubber gloves and mask, but special goggles and other new devices. Instead of the usual scaler, she told me in an excited voice how much better the new Cavitron with electromagnetic jet streams of pressurized water would clean my teeth.

Whatever, I thought to myself and hunkered down in the reclining chair with nervous anticipation. I kept debating with myself whether it was a good thing or a bad thing to have someone this new playing in my mouth. She would certainly be up on new technology and techniques, but then maybe she wouldn't have enough experience. I just wished she would stop jabbering about how wonderful my gums were.

I tuned her out as best I could, took a little nap with my mouth open, and then noticed she was asking me a question.

"How often do your brush your teeth?" she asked me in her eager, enthusiastic voice.

Was this a trick question, I wondered? No, I realized she was just going through the usual patient education spiel they teach them in dental hygiene school. Every 6 months we have to listen to these damn lectures about oral care. Hygienists don't seem to learn that patients don't listen, and even when we resolve to follow their instructions, the habits often don't stick for long. I have collected so many sets of gum stimulants, tongue brushers, and free samples of dental floss that I could open my own store.

"Twice a day," I finally answered her, convinced that was the right response.

She looked at me with worry. "Every day?" she asked again with doubt.

"Sure. Why? Is there some problem?"

Her face brightened. "No, not at all. Your oral hygiene is impeccable."

I tried to hide my pride. I was a veteran of periodontal surgery early in life, which got my attention to develop good brushing habits.

"What about flossing?" she asked me.

"What about it?"

She looked at me just the way a kindergarten teacher smiles indulgently at her rebellious children. "How often do you floss?"

"Every day," I said a little too quickly. That was a lie. The truth is that I didn't floss at all. I preferred toothpicks.

"Well, there is one spot here," she said as she stuck her finger in my mouth and touched the area under discussion, "where you are getting a little erosion."

I started to panic. I could picture having to go back under the gum knife again, probably the worst experience of my life. Talk about aversive conditioning.

The lecture soon ended. But something clicked inside my head. I knew at that moment that I would start flossing again, in addition to toothpicking. I was positive that this was not just an idle promise to myself; I knew that I was forever changed.

Of course, I would never have given the young woman the satisfaction of knowing that she had gotten through to me. In my mind, she was *way* too eager and bubbly as it was. I wouldn't want her to get the idea that she should keep badgering patients in that innocent, overly enthusiastic way.

She gave me my goodie bag filled with new samples of mouthwash, toothpaste, toothbrush, gum stimulators, a tongue cleaner, and some new products I had never seen before. Of course, there was dental floss as well. I said goodbye, scheduled a new appointment for 6 months hence, and walked out into the world.

Just as promised, I flossed that night, the night after that, and the one after that too. Hey, if we do something enough times, it becomes a habit, right?

So, why am I ending the book with this story?

As with other helping professionals, this hygienist had no idea that something she said or did impacted me in such a way that I changed my behavior, perhaps forever. Of course, it wasn't her efforts alone that made the difference—she merely triggered something that had been building within for some time which came together with other factors and influences at that moment.

I find it so interesting to deconstruct and analyze such helping encounters in order to make sense of what happened and why. What sticks out for me in this example is that we could theorize forever about the various possibilities and still never really know. Secondly, the person who helped me will never know.

☐ Epilogue to the Epilogue

One year later—still flossing.

REFERENCES

Abbey, E. (1990). *Desert solitaire*. New York: Touchstone.

Affleck, G., Tennen, H., Croog, S., & Levine, S. (1987). Causal attribution, perceived benefits, and morbidity after a heart attack: An 8-year study. *Journal of Consulting and Clinical Psychology, 55.* 29–35.

Aldwin, C. M. & Sutton, K. J. (1998). A developmental perspective on posttraumatic growth. In R. Tedeschi, C. Park, & L. Calhoun (Eds.), *Posttraumatic growth: Positive changes in the aftermath of crisis.* Mahway, NJ: Lawrence Erlbaum.

Alinsky, S. (1971/1993). Rules for radicals. *Columbia Dictionary of Quotations.* New York: Columbia University Press.

Allsop, S. & Saunders, B. (1989). Relapse and alcohol problems. In M. Gossop (Ed.), *Relapse and Addictive Behavior.* New York: Routledge.

Annis, H. K. (1986). A relapse prevention model for treatment of alcoholics. In D. Curson, H. Rankin & E. Shepherd (Eds.), *Relapse in alcoholism.* Northhampton, UK: Alcohol Counseling and Information Service.

Appelbaum, A. H. (1994). Psychotherapeutic routes to structural changes. *Bulletin of the Menninger Clinic, 58,* 37–54.

Asay, T. P. & Lambert, M. J. (1999). The empirical case for the common factors in therapy: Quantitative findings. In M. A. Hubble, B. L. Duncan, & S. D. Miller (Eds.), *The heart and soul of change.* Washington, DC: American Psychological Association.

Asher, S. J., Huffaker, G. Q., & McNally, M. (1994). Therapeutic considerations of wilderness experiences for incest and rape survivors. *Women and Therapy, 15.* 161–174.

Baldwin, J. (1977, December 19). Every good-bye ain't gone. *New York.*

Bandura, A. (1977). Self-efficacy: Toward a unifying theory of behavioral change. *Psychological Review, 84.* 191–215.

Bandura, A. (1997). *Self-efficacy.* New York: Freeman.

Bargh, J. A. & Chartrand, T. L. (1999). The unbearable automaticity of being. *American Psychologist, 54.* 462–479.

Bateson, G. (1972). *Steps to an ecology of mind.* New York: Dutton.

Baumeister, R. F. (1994). The crystallization of discontent in the process of major life change. In T. F. Heatherton & J. L. Weinberger (Eds.), *Can personality change?* Washington, DC: American Psychological Association.

Beck, A. (1997). Cognitive therapy: Reflections. In J. Zeig (Ed.), *The evolution of psychotherapy: The 3rd conference.* New York: Brunner/Mazel.

Beck, A. & Freeman, A. A. (1990). *Cognitive therapy of personality disorders.* New York: Guilford.

Becvar, D. S. & Becvar, R. J. (1988). *Family therapy: A systemic integration.* Boston: Allyn & Bacon.

Bohart, A. & Tallman, K. (1999). *How clients make therapy work: The process of active self-healing.* Washington, DC: American Psychological Association.

149

Boorstein, D. J. (1983). *The discoverers*. New York: Random House.

Brownell, K. D., Marlatt, G. A., Lichenstein, E., & Wilson, G. T. (1986). Understanding and preventing relapse. *American Psychologist, 4*. 765–782.

Bryson, B. (1998). *A walk in the woods: Rediscovering America on the Appalachian Trail*. New York: Broadway.

Buelow, G. D. & Buelow, S. A. (1998). *Psychotherapy in chemical dependence treatment*. Pacific Grove, CA: Brooks/Cole.

Bunker, B. B. & DeLisle, J. J. (1991). Individual change in organizational settings. In R. C. Curtis & G. Stricker (Eds.), *How people change: Inside and outside therapy*. New York: Plenum.

Cohen, L. H., Hettler, T. R., & Pane, N. (1998). Assessment of posttraumatic growth. In R. Tedeschi, C. Park, & L. Calhoun (Eds.), *Posttraumatic growth: Positive changes in the aftermath of crisis*. Mahway, NJ: Lawrence Erlbaum.

Collins, P. (1999). Eating disorders: A multiple-case investigation of the internet email correspondence of the daily lived experience of women (Doctoral dissertation, Texas Tech University, 1999). *Dissertation Abstracts International, ,.*

Cummings, A. L., Hallberg, E. T., & Selemon, A. G. (1994). Templates of client change in short-term counseling. *Journal of Counseling Psychology, 41*, 464–472.

Curtis, R. C. (1991). How people change: An introduction. In R. C. Curtis & G. Stricker (Eds.), *How people change: Inside and outside therapy*. New York: Plenum.

Curtis, R. C., & Stricker, G. (Eds.). (1991). *How people change: Inside and outside therapy*. New York: Plenum.

Dienstbier, R. A. (1992). Mutual impacts of toughening on crises and losses. In L. Montada, S. Filipp, & M. J. Lerner (Eds.), *Life crises and experiences of loss in adulthood* (pp. 367–384). Mahwah, NJ: Erlbaum.

Dweck, C. S. (1996). Implicit goals as organizers of goals and behavior. In P. M. Gollwitzer & J. A. Bargh (Eds.), *The psychology of action: Linking cognition and motivation to action*. New York: Guilford.

Ellis, A. (1995). *Better, deeper, and more enduring brief therapy: The rational emotive behavior therapy approach*. New York: Brunner/Mazel.

Ellis, A. (1997). Extending the goals of behavior therapy and of cognitive behavior therapy. *Behavior Therapy, 28*. 333–339.

Ellis, A. & MacLaren, C. (1998). *Rational emotive behavior therapy: A therapist's guide*. San Luis Obispo, CA: Impact Publishers.

Festinger, L. (1964). *Conflict, decision, and dissonance*. Palo Alto, CA: Stanford University Press.

Fimrite, R. (2000, July 10). Books. *Sports Illustrated*, 36.

Florian, V., Mikulincer, M., & Taubman, O. (1995). Does hardiness contribute to mental health during a stressful real-life situation? *Journal of Personality and Social Psychology, 68*. 687–695.

Frank, J. (1961). *Persuasion and healing*. Baltimore: Johns Hopkins Press.

Frank, J. & Frank, J. B. (1991). *Persuasion and healing* (3rd ed.). Baltimore: Johns Hopkins Press.

Fraser, K (1991). *Bad trips: A sometimes terrifying, sometimes hilarious collection of writing on the perils of the road*. New York: Vintage.

Gillis, H. L. & Simpson, C. (1991). Project choices: Adventure-based residential drug treatment for court-referred youth. *Journal of Addictions and Offender Counseling, 12*. 12–27.

Goldenberg, I. & Goldenberg, H. (2001). *Family therapy: An overview*. Pacific Grove, CA: Brooks/Cole.

Gollwitzer, P. M. (1999). Implementation intentions: Strong effects of simple plans. *American Psychologist, 54*. 493–503.

Gould, R. A. & Clum, G. A. (1993). A meta-analysis of self-help treatment approaches. *Clinical Psychology Review, 13.* 169–186.

Greenberg, L. S., Rice, L. N., & Elliott, R. (1993). *Facilitating emotional change: The moment-by-moment process.* New York: Guilford.

Greenberg, L. S. & Rhodes, R. H. (1991). Emotion in the change process. In R. C. Curtis & G. Stricker (Eds.), *How people change: Inside and outside therapy.* New York: Plenum.

Greenberg, L. S. & Safran, J. D. (1987). *Emotion in psychotherapy.* New York: Guilford.

Hager, D. (1992). Chaos and growth. *Psychotherapy, 29.* 378–384.

Haley, J. (1984). *Ordeal therapy: Unusual ways to change behavior.* San Francisco: Jossey-Bass.

Hall, S. K. (1999, September 6). I know that only cowards can be brave. *Newsweek,* 14.

Hanna, F. J. & Ritchie, M. H. (1995). Seeking the active ingredients of psychotherapeutic change: Within and outside the context of therapy. *Professional Psychology, 26.* 176–183.

Hart, B. H. L. (1954). *Strategy.* London: Faber & Faber.

Harvey, M. R. (1996). An ecological view of psychological trauma and trauma recovery. *Journal of Traumatic Stress, 9.* 3–23.

Havitz, M. E. & Howard, D. R. (1995). How enduring is enduring involvement? A seasonal examination of three recreational activities. *Journal of Consumer Psychology, 4.* 255–276.

Heat-Moon, W. L. (1999). *Blue highways: A journey into America.* Boston: Little, Brown.

Helson, R. & Stewart, A. (1994). Personality change in adulthood. In T. F. Heatherton & J. L. Weinberger (Eds.), *Can personality change?* Washington, DC: American Psychological Association.

Helson, R. & Wink, P. (1992). Personality change in women from early 40s to early 50s. *Psychology and Aging, 7.* 46–55.

Higgins, E. T. (1997). Beyond pleasure and pain. *American Psychologist, 52.* 1280–1300.

Holtzworth-Munroe, A. & Jacobson, N. S. (1985). Causal attributions of married couples: When do they search for causes? What do they conclude when they do? *Journal of Personality and Social Psychology, 57.* 967–980.

Hubble, M. A., Duncan, B. L., & Miller, S. D. (1999). *Heart and soul of change.* Washington, DC: American Psychological Association.

Hunt, W. A., Barnett, L. W., & Branch, L. G. (1971). Relapse rates in addiction programs. *Journal of Clinical Psychology, 27.* 455–456.

Irving, W. (1824/1993). Tales of a traveler. *Columbia Dictionary of Quotations.* New York: Columbia University Press.

Iyer, P. (2000). *The global soul: Jet lag, shopping malls, and the search for home.* New York: Knopf.

Jaffee, S. (1992). Pathways of relapse in adolescent chemical dependency recovery. *Adolescent Counselor, 55.* 42–44.

Johnson, S. M. (1996). *The practice of emotionally focused marital therapy.* New York: Brunner/Routledge.

Kaminer, W. (1992). *I'm dysfunctional, you're dysfunctional: The recovery movement and other self-help fashions.* Reading, MA: Addison-Wesley.

Kanfer, F. H. & Goldstein, A. P. (Eds.). (1986). *Helping people change* (3rd ed.). New York: Pergamon.

Keegan, P. (2000, March). No more mind games. *Outside,* 71–82.

Keniasty, K. & Norris, F. H. (1995). In search of altruistic community. *American Journal of Community Psychology, 23.* 447–477.

Kernberg, O. (1984). *Severe personality disorders.* New Haven, CT: Yale University Press.

Kingsolver, B. (1999). *The poisonwood bible.* New York: Harper Collins.

Kirschner, S. & Kirschner, D. A. (1991). The two faces of change: Progression and regression. In R. C. Curtis & G. Stricker (Eds.), *How people change: Inside and outside therapy.* New York: Plenum.

Kobasa, S. C. (1979). Stressful life events, personality, and health: An inquiry into hardiness. *Journal of Personality and Social Psychology, 37.* 1–11.

Kottler, J. A. (1986). *On being a therapist.* San Francisco: Jossey-Bass.

Kottler, J. A. (1991). *The compleat therapist.* San Francisco: Jossey-Bass.

Kottler, J. A. (1992). *Compassionate therapy: Working with difficult clients.* San Francisco: Jossey-Bass.

Kottler, J. A. (1993). *On being a therapist* (Rev. ed.). San Francisco: Jossey-Bass.

Kottler, J. A. (1995). *Growing a therapist.* San Francisco: Jossey-Bass.

Kottler, J. A. (1996). *Finding your way as a counselor.* Alexandria, VA: American Counseling Association.

Kottler, J. A. (1997). *Travel that can change your life.* San Francisco: Jossey-Bass.

Kottler, J. A. (1999). *The therapist's workbook.* San Francisco: Jossey-Bass.

Kottler, J. A. (2000a). The therapeutic benefits of structured travel experiences. *Journal of Activities in Psychotherapy Practice, 1.* 29–36.

Kottler, J. A. (2000b). Prescriptive travel and adventure-based activities as adjuncts to counselling. *Guidance and Counselling, 15.* 8–11.

Kottler, J. A. & Blau, D. S. (1989). *The imperfect therapist: Learning from failures in psychotherapy.* San Francisco: Jossey-Bass.

Kottler, J.A. & Hazler, R. (1997). *What you never learned in graduate school.* New York: Norton.

Kottler, J. A., Sexton, T., & Whiston, S. (1994). *Heart of healing: Relationships in therapy.* San Francisco: Jossey-Bass.

Krakauer, J. (1997). *Into the wild.* New York: Bantam.

Kuhn, T. S. (1962). *The structure of scientific revolutions.* Chicago: University of Chicago Press.

Lambert, M. J. (1992). Implications of outcome research for psychotherapy integration. In J. C. Norcross and M. R. Goldfried (Eds.), *Handbook of psychotherapy integration.* New York: Basic Books.

Lambert, M. J. & Bergin, A. E. (1994). The effectiveness of psychotherapy. In A. E. Bergin & S. L. Garfield (Eds.), *Handbook of psychotherapy and behavior change* (4th ed.). New York: Wiley.

Lapierre, D. (1985). *The city of joy.* New York: Warner.

Laws, D. R. (1995). A theory of relapse prevention. In W. O'Donahue and L. Krasner (Eds.), *Theories of behavior therapy.* Washington, DC: American Psychological Association.

Laws, D. R. (1999). Relapse prevention: The state of the art. *Journal of Interpersonal Violence, 14.* 285–302.

Lebow, J. (1999). Seven principles of performance enhancement. *Family Therapy Networker,* 32–34.

Locke, E. A. & Latham, G. P. (1990). *A theory of goal setting and task performance.* Englewood Cliffs, NJ: Prentice Hall.

Ludgate, J. W. (1995). *Maximizing psychotherapeutic gains and preventing relapse in emotionally distressed clients.* Sarasota, FL: Professional Resource Press.

Lyddon, W. J. (1990). First- and second-order change: Implications for rationalist and constructivist cognitive therapies. *Journal of Counseling and Development, 69.* 122–127.

Mahoney, M. J. (1991). *Human change processes.* New York: Wiley.

Mahoney, M. J. (1997). Brief moments and enduring effects: Reflections on time and timing in psychotherapy. In W. J. Matthews, (Eds.), *Current thinking and research in brief therapy: Solutions, strategies, narratives.* New York: Brunner/Mazel.

Mahrer, A. (1985). *Psychotherapeutic change: An alternative approach to meaning and measurement.* New York: Norton.

Marlatt, G. A. & Gordon, J. R. (1985). *Relapse prevention: Maintenance strategies in the treatment of addictive behaviors.* New York: Guilford.

Martin, J. (1994). *The construction and understanding of psychotherapeutic change.* New York: Teachers College Press.

McAlpine, K. (1999, October). Eat no evil. *Spirit,* 72–77.

McMillen, C., Zuravin, S., & Rideout, G. (1995). Perceived benefits from child sexual abuse. *Journal of Consulting and Clinical Psychology, 63.* 1037–1043.

Meichenbaum, D. (1985). *Stress inoculation training.* New York: Pergamon.

Mermelstein, R. J., Karantz, T., & Reichmann, S. (1992). Smoking. In P. H. Wilson (Ed.), *Principles and practice of relapse prevention.* New York: Guilford.

Miller, I. W. (1984). Strategies for maintenance of treatment gains for depressed patients. *The Cognitive Behaviorist, 6.* 10–13.

Miller, W. R. & C'deBaca, J. (1994). Quantum change: Toward a psychology of transformation. In T. F. Heatherton & J. L. Weinberger (Eds.), *Can personality change?* Washington, DC: American Psychological Association.

Monk, G., Winslade, J., Crocket, K., & Epston, D. (1997). *Narrative therapy in practice.* San Francisco: Jossey-Bass.

Neimeyer, R. A. (1995). An invitation to constructivist psychotherapies. In R. A. Neimeyer & M. J. Mahoney (Eds.), *Constructivism in psychotherapy.* Washington, DC: American Psychological Association.

Nelson, C. & Jackson, P. (1989). High-risk recognition: The cognitive-behavioral chain. In D. R. Laws (Ed.), *Relapse prevention with sex offenders.* New York: Guilford.

Nim, H. (1985). Mood disorders: pharmacological prevention of recurrences. *American Journal of Psychiatry, 142.* 469–476.

Norcross, J. C. & Goldfried, M. R. (Eds.). (1992). *Handbook of psychotherapy integration.* New York: Basic Books.

Norcross, J. C., Ratzin, A. C., & Payne, D. (1989). Ringing in the New Year: The change processes and reported outcomes of resolutions. *Addictive Behaviors, 14.* 205–212.

O'Leary, V. E. & Ickovics, J. R. (1995). Resilience and thriving in response to challenge: An opportunity for a paradigm shift in women's health. *Women's Health: Research on Gender, Behavior, and Policy, 1.* 121–142.

Park, D. C. (1999). Acts of will? *American Psychologist, 54.* 461.

Patton, W. & McMahon, M. (1999). *Career development and systems theory: A new synthesis.* Pacific Grove, CA: Brooks/Cole.

Pirsig, R. M. (1974). *Zen and the art of motorcycle maintenance.* New York: Bantam.

Pithers, W. D. (1991). Relapse prevention with sexual aggressors. *Forum on Corrections Research, 3.* 20–23.

Presbyterian Healthcare Services (1999). *Tips for keeping your New Year's resolutions.* [on-line] Available: www.phs.org/healthyliving/tips/.

Prochaska, J. & DiClemente, C. (1986). Toward a comprehensive model of change. In W. Miller & N. Heather (Eds.), *Treating Addictive Behavior.* New York: Plenum.

Prochaska, J. O., Norcross, J. C., & DiClemente, C. C. (1994). *Changing for good.* New York: Morrow.

Prochaska, J. O. (1999). How do people change, and how can we change to help many more people? In M. A. Hubble, B. L. Duncan, & S. D. Miller (Eds.), *The heart and soul of change.* Washington, DC: American Psychological Association.

Robbins, T. (1976). *Even cowgirls get the blues.* New York: Bantam.

Rogers, R. L. & McMillin, C. S. (1992). *Relapse traps.* New York: Bantam.

Rutter, M. (1987). Psychosocial resilience and protective mechanisms. *American Journal of Orthopsychiatry, 57.* 316–331.

Schaefer, J. A. & Moos, R. H. (1998). The context for posttraumatic growth. In R. Tedeschi, C. Park, & L. Calhoun (Eds.), *Posttraumatic growth: Positive changes in the aftermath of crisis.* Mahway, NJ: Erlbaum.

Scogin, F., Bynum, J., Stephens, G., & Cahoon, S. (1990). Efficacy of self-administered treatment programs: Meta-analytic review. *Professional Psychology: Research and Practice, 21.* 42–47.

Shiffman, S. (1992). Relapse process and relapse prevention in the addictive behaviors. *The Behavior Therapist, 15.* 9–11.

Snyder, C. R., Michael, S. T., & Cheavens, J. S. (1999). Hope as a psychotherapeutic foundation of common factors, placebos, and expectancies. In M. A. Hubble, B. L. Duncan, & S. D. Miller (Eds.), *The heart and soul of change.* Washington, DC: American Psychological Association.

Spense, D. P. (1982). *Narrative and historical truth.* New York: Norton.

Spiegler, M. D. & Guevremont, D. C. (1998). *Contemporary behavior therapy.* Pacific Grove, CA: Brooks/Cole.

Sulzer-Azaroff, B. & Mayer, G. R. (1991). *Behavior analysis for lasting change.* Fort Worth: Holt, Rinehart, and Winston.

Swan, G. E. & Denk, C. E. (1987). Dynamic models for maintenance of smoking cessation: Event history analysis of late relapse. *Journal of Behavioral Medicine, 10.* 527–554.

Tallman, K. & Bohart, A. C. (1999). The client as a common factor: Clients as self-healers. In M. A. Hubble, B. L. Duncan, & S. D. Miller (Eds.), *The heart and soul of change.* Washington, DC: American Psychological Association.

Tedeschi, R. G., Park, C. L., & Calhoun, L. G. (Eds.). (1998). *Posttraumatic growth: Positive changes in the aftermath of crisis.* Mahwah, NJ: Erlbaum.

Texas Medical Association (1999). *Keeping your New Year's resolutions.* [on-line] Available: www.texmed.org/health.

Thayer, H. (1993). *Polar dreams: The heroic saga of the first solo journey by a woman and her dog to the Pole.* New York: Delta.

Tyler, A. (1985). *The accidental tourist.* New York: Berkley.

Tyler, A. (1988). *Breathing lessons.* New York: Knopf.

Vaughan, D. (1986). *Uncoupling.* New York: Oxford University Press.

von Bertalanffy, L. (1968). *General systems theory.* New York: Braziller.

Wachtel, P. L. (1991). The role of accomplices in preventing and facilitating change. In R. C. Curtis & G. Stricker (Eds.), *How people change: Inside and outside therapy.* New York: Plenum.

Wallerstein, J. S. (1986). Women after divorce: Preliminary report of a 10-year follow-up. *American Journal of Orthopsychiatry, 56.* 65–77.

Wallerstein, R. S. (1986). *Forty two lives in treatment.* New York: Guilford.

Wanigaratne, S., Wallace, W., Pullin, J., Kearney, F., & Farmer, R. (1990). *Relapse prevention for addictive behaviours.* Oxford: Blackwell.

Watzlawick, P., Weakland, J., & Fisch, R. (1974). *Change: Principles of problem formation and problem resolution.* New York: Norton.

Weathers, B. (2000). *Left for dead: My journey home from Everest.* New York: Villard.

Weil, A. (1995). *Health and healing.* Boston: Houghton Mifflin.

Wiener, N. (1954). *Cybernetics.* Cambridge, MA: MIT Press.

White, M. & Epston, D. (1990). *Narrative means to therapeutic ends.* New York: Norton.

Wilson, P. H. (1992). *Principles and practice of relapse prevention.* New York: Guilford.

Zenmore, R. & Shepel, L. F. (1989). Effects of breast cancer and mastectomy on emotional support and adjustment. *Social Science and Medicine, 28.* 19–27.

Zukav, G. (1979). *The dancing Wu Li masters.* New York: Bantam.

Zurick, D. (1995). *Errant journeys: Adventure travel in a modern age.* Austin: University of Texas Press.

INDEX

('f' indicates a figure; 't' indicates a table)

155

ABOUT
THE AUTHOR

Jeffrey A. Kottler is one of the most prolific authors in the field. He has authored a dozen texts for counselors, teachers, and therapists (e.g., *Introduction to Therapeutic Counseling*, 4th Edition; *Advanced Group Leadership*, 2nd Edition; *Counseling Skills for Teachers*, 2nd Edition) and another dozen books on the nature of change (e.g., *On Being a Therapist, What You Never Learned in Graduate School, Growing a Therapist*), and teaching (e.g., *On Being a Teacher, Classrooms Under the Influence, Succeeding With Difficult Students*). He has also authored several trade books which describe complex phenomena in highly accessible prose (*Travel That Can Change Your Life, Private Moments, Secret Selves, The Language of Tears*). The present work is the sequel to a previous Brunner-Routledge book (*Doing Good: Passion and Commitment For Helping Others*).

Jeffrey has been an educator for 25 years. He has worked as a teacher, counselor, and therapist in preschool, middle school, mental health center, crisis center, university, community college, and private practice settings. He has served as a Fulbright Scholar and Senior Lecturer in Peru (1980) and Iceland (2000), as well as having worked in numerous countries as a consultant and trainer specializing in multicultural issues.

Jeffrey is currently Chair of the Counseling Department at California State University, Fullerton.